STORIES of the
UNSEEN

Praise for *Stories of the Unseen* from Around the World

"Whether you believe in ghosts or not, these stories might change your mind about them! Selena tells us in clear words that magic is all around us, and in what ways entities contribute to our lives." - Yvonne Gerner, Norway

"This book is a travel-like treasure hunt. Enticing. Challenging. Candid. Powerful. Healing. Nurturing. The stories are just enough to invite you to immerse yourself in the energies and for you to start asking yourself questions. It pulls down the undies of any monster and shows a light, funny, sometimes childlike wonder of this overmystified and yet so little explored world. Such a magical book!" - Oana Merisescu, Romania

"These unveiling stories take you to mysterious places, forgotten times, and everyday scenes. The author's finely honed honesty and on point dialogue made me savour the unseen in a renewed way. Illuminating!" - Freeke Carlier, Belgium

"This book is a game changer! Before reading this book, I thought I knew about entities and how to deal with them. I had no idea the extent they are present in our daily lives and how recognizing their presence makes life so much easier! I have a much greater awareness of entities now and, as a result, a much greater sense of myself."- Fay Thompson, Canada

"Reading this was a delicious experience. The subject of entities can be a challenge to write about, but Selena turns each chapter into a vivid, colorful, and captivating story creating a sense of intimacy and vulnerability that pulls you in and makes you want to read more. Thank you Selena for choosing to write and for being an inspiration. It brought me comfort to know that my awareness is okay and does not need to be hidden." – Aysegul Sevil, Turkey

STORIES of the
UNSEEN

Selena Ardelean

Copyright© 2021 Selena Ardelean
Cover Design: Sandra Schoenmakers

Published by: Big Moose Publishing
PO Box 127 Site 601 RR#6 Saskatoon, SK CANADA S7K3J9
www.bigmoosepublishing.com

All rights reserved. No part of this book may be used or reproduced by any means, graphic, electronic, or mechanical, including photocopying, recording, taping or by any information storage retrieval system without the written permission of the author except in the case of brief quotations embodied in critical articles and reviews.

Because of the dynamic nature of the Internet, any web addresses or links contained in this book may have changed since publication and may no longer be valid. The views expressed in this work are solely those of the author and do not necessarily reflect the views of the publisher, and the publisher hereby disclaims any responsibility for them.

The author of this book does not dispense medical advice or prescribe the use of any technique as a form of treatment for physical, emotional, or medical problems without the advice of a physician, either directly or indirectly. The intent of the author is only to offer information of a general nature to help you in your quest for emotional and spiritual well-being. In the event you use any of the information in this book for yourself, which is your constitutional right, the author and the publisher assume no responsibility for your actions.

ISBN: 978-1-989840-23-8(softcover)
ISBN: 978-1-989840-24-5(ebook)

Big Moose Publishing 06/2021

*With gratitude to ALL who walk the path towards
being more of who they are:
weird, beautiful, different and amazing, seen and unseen,
embodied or disembodied.*

Thank you for our ongoing unfolding journey together.

Table of Contents

Foreword 1
Who's Afraid of Entities? 7
Shining in the Ardennes 11
The Chapel 24
A Gift from Earth 30
The Old Woman with Milky Blue Eyes 36
Asking for a Miracle 40
The Cherry Tree 48
Beings of Light 54
Golden Wings 59
Birthday Wish 68
Malaysian Airlines 77
Sugar High 82
The Lady in the Channel 88
Snuffy 92
Helga 102
I Love Brazil 111
Entities of the Earth 122
Russia 127
Paris 136

Greece……………………………………………………………144
The Isle of the Bloody Ones……………………………152
All Roads Lead to Rome…………………………………169
Turkey……………………………………………………………179
Anubis……………………………………………………………186
Pearls for Girls………………………………………………192
India………………………………………………………………202
Mexico……………………………………………………………222
Afterword………………………………………………………237
End Notes………………………………………………………243
About the Author……………………………………………245

Foreword

I have never truly understood what the function of a foreword written by an author was.

It was the part of a book that I would usually skip, because I didn't want anyone to influence my reading, not even the writer himself. I've always been a rebellious reader, demanding my freedom to gallop over the pages and envision the story myself. Whomever the person behind the penning of the lines was, the universe of the book opened up and landed in my world in a totally different way. For me, reading a book is to watch a film woven from images, perceptions, sensations, thoughts, feelings, and emotions completely unique to me. My reading would always glide behind the lines, inquiring the non-said and the non-seen.

This is what I would like to encourage you to do with this book. Read, dive, and know there's a whole unseen world waiting for you to discover and receive in each paragraph. Allow these stories to be a key to the realm of the unseen world that has always been present in your life, tickling you to notice. These *Stories of the Unseen* will not give you answers, but they will invite you to ask two questions: "What am I aware of?" and "What is true for me?"

I have written the stories in this book at different stages of my life. I was never alone when I birthed them. Some have waited for years to be put on paper as I made them way too significant when they occurred. That, or I was unaware of the true beauty these experiences were bringing to the surface. It took time for me to realize they required to be shared. Others are very recent, and poured into my life with my choice to write this book. It's as if they were demanding to be included in these pages.

I have used various tools for accessing the unseen world throughout the course of my life. All had their part to play. Yet, the biggest expansion in this exploration was ignited by the tools of Talk To The Entities®[1], created by Shannon O'Hara, and the body of work of Access Consciousness®[2], founded by

Stories of the Unseen

Gary Douglas and Dr. Dain Heer. They truly invited me to know what I know beyond significance, fear, doubt, or limitation. And I am asking you in turn: "What do you know?"

Let your curiosity without judgment and your quest for more consciousness lead you. Follow the energy and allow the magic contribution of the feather-like presence of entities in your life be an invitation to be more of who you are. Opening up to the spirit world, regardless the method, the way, or the rituals you are using, is an invaluable gift. It is a demand from yourself to trust you and what you have always known possible with the spirit world, even if you have never had words for it.

You, my dear friend, have always been aware of entities. You cannot *not* be aware. You can muffle your capacities, but you cannot get rid of them. They are part of who you are. You've been aware of entities for lifetimes. Your body has been primed to receive information from the *unseen*. This is not new to you. What if you knew that it is only you in the entire world who knows what you know, and that you are an invaluable spark of magic that shifts realities through your capacity of communicating with the entities? What if you allowed yourself to discover what else is truly possible beyond what your mind tries to control and has defined as impossible?

Everything that you make significant limits your capacity to perceive what is true for you. Awareness is light, quicksilver, and ethereal. Significance slows life down and forges it into concrete boxes. It forces you into taking things for granted.

Being aware of entities is an invitation to question what seems to be and to allow more of who you be in your life. It's a trust-in-yourself exercise. It's a continuous question: "What am I aware of?"

Awareness is not personal. It's not about who you are and what you do. It doesn't mean anything. It's not significant. It's an energetic doorway to a possibility that has not yet existed. You are the only one capable of grasping it. You are the only one capable of walking through the doorway presented to you.

This book is primarily about igniting a sparkle of curiosity towards the unseen world and the entities that occupy that world.

So, what is an entity?

A song is an entity. A relationship is an entity. An obsessive idea, a limitation, an emotion… they are all entities. A person who has left their body is an entity. A fairy, a tree, demons, angels, Beings of

Light, and your house are all entities. You are an embodied entity.

There has never been any separation between you and the entity world other than the things you believed in or not. What if instead of believing, you could simply know?

Your awareness is yours only and solely unique to you. No one in this world can come and invalidate your awareness. Trust yours even when it doesn't make sense from a logical point of view. If you're wondering whether you're inventing things, ask yourself: Am I expanded or contracted? Am I happy, light, carefree, joyful, and grateful or heavy, slow, and bored?

What is true for you will always make you feel lighter, giggly, expanded, and at peace. A lie will make you feel heavy and contracted.

Follow your truth!

And, if you are making things up? Would you allow yourself to step beyond the threshold of control and soar in a realm where not many dare venture without drama and trauma and suffering? Will you be the one who curiously questions all the myths and legends that keep you from enjoying your awareness? I wonder how much more you know about entity awareness that you have not allowed yourself to acknowledge up until now?

The anecdotes and stories I share in this book, though inspired from my own life, are mere instances pinned in time. They can be shuffled and maybe, by the time you read them, they will have already shifted and transformed energies by you merely acknowledging the presence of the unseen among us. Allow yourself to acknowledge those instances in your life as well, so that any heavy energies can dissipate and leave your universe. This usually happens easily once you choose to shake off the significance of your findings.

Last, but not least, choose ease with your awareness. Make a demand of yourself to keep asking questions and have fun!

What if you allowed yourself, for a few pages, to savour all your knowing you've been harnessing for millions of years, and acknowledge the whispers and subtle touches of the unseen in your daily life?

Would you allow yourself the childish curiosity of exploring, discovering, and acknowledging the presence of entities in your life regardless of the method, the technique, or the tools you use to do so?

Who's Afraid of Entities?

Are you afraid of entities? Well, I get you! I used to be afraid of them too. I mean… I used to be afraid of the stories that I heard about them from my grandmother, my friends, horror movies, and the haunted houses series on some weird TV channels. I would not have watched one second of those movies unless I stumbled upon them accidentally. And yet I have always been fascinated by the spirit world, even if it wasn't clear for me what that truly meant.

I was around 10 years old in communist Romania when anything about the spirit world or religion was banned from peoples' lives. It was forbidden to go to church; therefore, praying and worshipping was done behind closed doors in huge secrecy. This also led to derivative practices overloaded with significance.

I remember that we were not allowed to have a Christmas tree in the house and the visits of "the Security" to the house, because 'glimmering lights' had caught the eye of someone from the street. My father used to be an important figure in the Communist Party back then; therefore, he was closely monitored in his activities. Even though we were not allowed to talk about spirit, my father was the first one who taught me to never settle on only what the eyes could see, and to stretch my logic out until something else other than cause and effect could reach my world.

He was a psychologist, and keenly interested in paranormal activities, telepathy, and scientific studies of the mind. He was bold and rebellious, and he instilled curiosity in my world, even if it meant that one day he would not come home any more. The stories of members of families disappearing and being imprisoned without further notice by the Militia were not a myth. They were happening. The general state of being at that time was fear.

I grew up with that fear and with the responsibility

to always be on the lookout, to mind what I was saying, and to pay attention to whom I was talking to or telling my stories, so that it would not harm my family. In the end, fear took over and the fascination with the paranormal experiments my father was sharing with me faded into the woodwork. Instead, I became an impetuous teenager fighting against any form of control.

Despite all that, years later when my father died, I embraced his death with serenity and peace. He died in the hospital after a severe stroke. I was on a train to a different city when he went into a coma. The situation looked pretty grim, but I knew he would wait until I returned. 24 hours later I was in the hospital ward telling him for the first time that I loved him. He was dying and I was willing to let him go.

The morning he died I stepped into the hospital ward and I had this clear perception that he was no longer in his body. He kind of watched me from above. I was not scared; I was not frantic. I was at peace. I knew he was "waiting" for me before he left for good. When his body failed to breathe, I apologized for not being able to see him pass. I know as I know the sun rises in the morning that when I stepped out of the room, his body died.

And while I was stepping out, a chariot full of newborn babies was being carried from the delivery room just across the hallway. "One out, plenty in," a voice resonated in my head.

For years I thought I was imagining it - that it was something my mind fabricated to keep me afloat - to protect me from the sorrow. Yet, the calm and composure I perceived coming with this message allowed me to navigate my father's dying with ease.

It's been 14 years since his death, and in all these years, he has visited me only once in my dreams, immediately after the burial service. I had been crying for days, consumed with guilt feelings that I should have fought more for him, while knowing that this was his choice. He was a strong, potent, stubborn man. His choice to leave had been clear for a while preceding his actual death.

He visited me with my old dog, Dolly, and then they moved on. It was all I required to let me know that it was time for me to move on as well.

Shining in the Ardennes

I was taking refuge in a hotel in the Ardennes. See, I was going through a particularly rough patch with my business. I had watched my creations go to the slaughterhouse one by one and I couldn't bring myself to do anything about them. I mourned them, but I was more upset about all my expectations being blown away than I was about the disappearing of what I had called 'my great creations'.

They had never been mine to start with. What if their death was actually their contribution in my life? And what if whenever one creation dies, it is actually transmuting into a higher form of presence and new creation? Wouldn't that be easier on all the magnificent creators who follow the cortege of deceased ideas to the bottom of a bottle of wine or to the last cigarette in the pack?

What if these creations were an invitation to let go of control, to be present, and to ask one vital question: "Who does this belong to?" It's not the death of an idea that saddens us. It's the frustration that it chose to die when we had all our hopes and dreams up... as if the death of a creation says anything about us, about who we are, how worthy we are, or the limits of what we could ask for.

So there I was, alone in the Belgian Ardennes, licking my creative wounds, away from my comfortable white chair and my cosy office, in an ancient hotel that used to be part of a church in the Middle Ages. It was just me, my laptop, a candle, my favourite notebook, two books, something to munch on, and a bottle of red wine.

I felt hurt and disappointed, and on top of it all, I had just terminated what I affectionately called "my team." I had called in defeat and concluded I was not a good leader after all. My shoulders stiffened with the heaviness of the guilt and the shame I had been building up for not having been able to get things right. Those three days of solitude were meant to bring me closer to who I was, regardless of what this world considered a success or a failure.

It was in the isolation from the roaring judgments of the world, in the deep thick silence of a frozen village in the Belgian Ardennes, that I asked to be shown what was true about me. I wanted to finally see what lies I had believed were real, which in turn kept me away from what I knew beyond a shadow of doubt that was true.

At first it was exciting – one night alone, no calls, no zooms, and no one around. Me, my candle, soft ambient music, a glass of wine, a great book and… No. That wasn't my way. I soon found out that this silence wasn't what I was looking for. In fact, as it often happens, you don't quite know what you're looking for until you find it.

My silent retreat coincided with the full moon. It was shining round and fat above the silent village as if hanging on the tower of the church next to my hotel. It mesmerized me. It was as if I had been doing this, gazing at the moon from my hotel room, many times before.

I lay in bed listening to Gregorian music and I closed my eyes for a few moments.

It felt as if I had plunged centuries back in history and I was part of the nuns worshipping their saint in the church that used to be this hotel. I could smell the candles, the myrrh balm, and the rose perfume.

I perceived a restlessness there, as if there was something else which I was aware of but could not put any words to it. A presence. Yes. I could tell there was a feminine presence, somewhere to my left. She was holding her hands in humble prayer, her head down, and waiting for me to see her.

"Hello…" I whispered.

The nun lifted her head. I could not see her face. I just had a glimpse of the white band on the forehead showing from under her headscarf. In a fraction of a second the information reached me as if poured in by the bucket. She spoke fast in half phrases. My head interfered willing to have the whole story in an ordered way. I reminded myself that this was not the point.

"Can I help you?" I asked. She was ashamed and prayed for deliverance, which she didn't think she deserved.

She had dedicated her life to pray for forgiveness, because she fell in love with a young man who came to work in the village. She sinned, and her family forced her to go to the convent. She knew she didn't deserve absolution, but she thought that praying and being loyal to the church would finally allow her to go to heaven.

"Oh, would you like to go to heaven?" I asked in my mind. A draught of fear reached up to me.

"It's all right," I said. "Do you know that you died? That you don't have a body any longer?"

The nun seemed puzzled and disturbed. This information didn't exist in her world up until that moment.

She nodded.

"Who are you?" There was silence.

Simply by asking this question, I could perceive her confusion dissipating. All this time she thought she had no other choice than keep repenting for her sins. It seemed that she had stepped into a swirl of other past lifetimes and saw that she could actually choose to move on.

I must have fallen asleep. When I woke up I was trembling on the bed. It was cold. I looked at the clock. 3:03 am. I tucked myself under the covers with a large smile on my face. It had been a fabulous day in the entity world, and one of them had made a different choice. What a gift!

I woke up the next morning feeling strangely relieved, but with visible signs of entity awareness on my face. My eyes were puffy, my lips were dry, and my hair looked as if someone had played with it the whole night.

I smiled while brushing my teeth and preparing to get out of the room. I had breakfast and then went for a walk. There was a 6km walking trail in the countryside that my body was eager to take. The snow was inviting me to explore the cold heights of the Ardennes at a friendly pace. I put on my boots, and I rushed out in the frozen scenery.

The beauty of the snow melting from the trees invited me to explore my walk differently. I had been questioning myself for a while. I wondered, "What did *Shine* really mean to me?" That was my catch phrase: Shine. Since one of the classes I created around the topic of "shining" was cancelled, I judged the hell out of it and me.

Still, there I was, with a narrow muddy path under my feet requiring me to be present with my body and the slippery steps. My whole body was contracted in an attempt to not fall in the dirt puddles where my feet sunk in the mud up to my ankles.

A single thought crossed my mind. "I was inspired to take these boots with me!"

My body sighed. Yes, my body already knew about my adventure. This was probably why I got the ping to take my boots on the journey, even though I had not worn them for years. I also realized that I was not being present. My body was nudging me towards that. I was focusing so much on what might happen if I were not paying attention, that I was excluding my body entirely from the computation. Because of this, I continuously kept my head down ignoring the gorgeousness of the fields in front of me that were covered in shimmering snow.

"Let's rest," I told my body. "No one is rushing us back to the hotel room. What if we just enjoyed this?"

I found a pile of logs and sat down. The immensity of the nature embraced me. There was a painting-like clear blue sky, a fluffy white cushion of snow, my black jacket, and my rich red shawl gently blowing in the wind. The sound of ice melting from the branches of the forest trees echoed in my ears. My body shrugged with the surprise of this somewhat familiar noise coming to us from across lifetimes.

My feet were playing with the mud. My back was leaning against the pile of wet tree trunks. It smelled like fresh cut wood almost making me want to have a taste of the bark. I closed my eyes and took a deep breath. Then another one. My shoulders dropped; my neck relaxed. My hands were dropping next to my body.

"Mmmmmhhhh…"

I heard a whisper close to me, soft and clear, sounding like a voice (although it wasn't): "This is shine." The message spread itself throughout my entire body as if to remind all the cells and molecules that shine is where I am, in communion with it all, with the skies, with the forest, with the mud, with the mountains, with the elementals, with the wood…

When I opened my eyes, my vision seemed clearer and sharper. A million sparkles of awareness stormed into my world tickling my seriousness away. My body felt lighter and uplifted. My feet were carrying me effortlessly on the rough path. I didn't have to worry. All that was required of me was to… receive. It felt as if I were floating above the gliding path.

From time to time, huge pine trees would shed ice diamonds from their branches that were shining bright in the sunlight. I was now walking straight with open arms, smiling childishly. The smell of the pine trees reminded me of Christmas. I just wished I could have had a branch to put in my hotel room. It would have been such a sweet reminder of this adventure.

Just then, a small branch landed at my feet. It had two pine cones attached to it.

"Thank you!" I shouted. I knew I was watched over and that there were many entities playing with me. All I had to be was the joy of receiving the gifts from beyond what met the eyes and to be the spoiled little kid who plays with the wonders of the unseen world. Nothing more…

The time was flowing by. It was early afternoon and I still had a few kilometres to walk back to the hotel. I had been walking for almost 3 hours, yet I knew that my time didn't match what this world referenced as time. To me it was a mere indication of how the sun was moving on the horizon. My adventure was more like stepping into a different dimension where time was not relevant.

I noticed that when the road did a large turn to the

left, I began snapping out of the bliss. It was as if the sadness of this world was catching up with me. The road in front of me had been hardly walked on. I could appreciate that I was getting closer to the village by the uneasiness and melancholy I could feel ahead.

All of a sudden a grey emptiness covered my joy like a choking blanket. I wanted to sit down and cry, as if I had lost something precious and beloved. There was a pain squeezing my heart… and sorrow, and longing, and despair, and…

I sunk my face deep in the snow that covered a stump of a tree that had been cut at waist height, on the side of the road. My cheeks were on fire; my eyes were swollen. I numbed the intense sudden suffering by holding my breath with my head buried deep in the icy snow cushion. It felt good, until I started to choke and breathe in heavily.

"Oh, so I panic now? What is this?" I demanded lifting my head and looking around. The cemetery of the village was only 50 metres in the distance, protected by a high cement fence from any unwanted intruders. And there was something else.

Tall, in uniform, sad, in despair, waiting powerless… an officer from World War II. I swallowed in disbelief at first and forced all my barriers down. I could perceive his refrained sobbing and sorrow.

"Hello." I whispered towards the presence standing next to a grave.

My heart started to race. I was cold. The information poured in… died in war, lover didn't come to visit him, he was missing her, why? What did he do? She promised she would come every day…

I wasn't sure what I was supposed to do. Could I talk to ghosts just like that? Most of the time they sought me, but this time… I perceived him. It felt as if I was barging into a private setting, yet I somehow knew he was connected to me. I didn't think. I just asked.

"Sir, do you know that you died?"

"Yes. I was shot in my heart and my chest."

"Do you know that you can leave your grave and go look for your love?"

This question of mine was met with his utter disbelief and curiosity.

"You know… it's been a long time… Maybe your sweetheart died as well. Maybe you could meet her on the other side? Or choose to take a new body and experience life on Earth again?"

It was the first time that I had such a vivid encounter with an entity, and I realized that my curiosity took over any hesitation I had.

"What would you like to choose? Would you like to be freed from your grave?" I perceived his confused surprise. He didn't know he could leave his grave.

He agreed and left.

I realized that all along during this energetic exchange the wind had stopped blowing. It was like we were frozen in one capsule of memory together. Immediately after clearing this entity, a gush of wind forced me to take shelter under a huge tree that I had not seen before. I wondered if it wasn't the tree where they used to meet as he kept staring in its direction.

My walk odyssey seemed to reach an end. The first houses of the village appeared and the path opened into a paved road. The thoughts of those in businesses nearby filled in my ears with the well-known background of rushing ideas, which I was used to being aware of in other peoples' worlds.

Stories of the Unseen

Back in my hotel room I wrote in my notebook: what if *shining* is about being yourself beyond the thoughts and expectations of this busy and limited world? What if my business shines when I choose to shine?

The Chapel

It's late afternoon. Snuffy, my dog, is waiting for me impatiently. I promised her we would go on a walk in the forest, our "magic forest." It's a place we go to where no judgment survives, where worries dissolve, where sorrow melts. It's a miraculous place where I can enjoy being me, whoever I choose to be.

We have our own path and a hidden entrance to the domain of the "Three Fountains." We adore exploring its treasures and encountering its beings. It's a habit to say 'hi' to the birds, the rabbits, the foxes, the squirrels, and to all the unseen presences walking next to us.

In my magic forest there is an old deserted chapel.

It used to belong to the royal domain. There is also what was once a fancy mansion that now has been restored to a restaurant. Some other buildings in the vicinity have been converted from stalls into children activity spaces.

There is also a huge spacious lawn in the middle of the trees that is busily populated by kids during the summer. The whole setting is great for nature discovery, treasure hunts, boy scout games, and all kinds of other adventures.

Almost every wall of these half abandoned buildings is tagged in some way. There are splashes of paintball fights and primitive huts made of branches for taking shelter on rainy days.

I am walking my dog, or maybe she is walking me. We are not quite sure who's leading whom while walking, when my attention is suddenly pulled towards the white deserted chapel on top of the hill, somewhat secluded from the uproar on the lawn.

I've passed by this chapel the whole summer, because there was something telling me that my trespassing was not welcome. I would get shivers down my spine or I would change direction as if by a strange coincidence so that I would not step into that space. I knew it was there; I could see it. Still, it seemed as if it didn't exist. My dog would not get closer either.

Today, it is different. I stepped straight towards it and I touched the walls. I walked around it, keeping my palm on the cold orange bricks. Soon I was standing in front of the entrance staring through the bars of a heavy black iron door. The metal gate must have replaced a wooden one in order to prevent vandalism. It's funny how humans cannot stand closed doors, just like cats… for totally different reasons though.

The interior had been renovated not too long ago judging from the almost-white paint on the walls. It had all its windows intact. Sunlight was coming through the glass that replaced once beautifully crafted stained glass. Light rays waved in front of me while bathing the empty altar. There were all kind of bottles and cans on the ground mingled with dead leaves from the autumn winds. The air was cold. It smelled somehow like my grandmother's roof closet, the one I was not allowed to touch, and that I was afraid to be next to when I was a child.

My grandmother's roof was forbidden territory. She must have had her reasons. A lot of family stuff since the death of her husband had been stored in the attic. In my head there must have been something dangerous up there.

Once I sneaked out my grandmother's supervision and I climbed the stairs that she had somehow left unattended. I couldn't see much. It was pitch dark and among the complete havoc of things piled up one on top the other, a trunk popped just in front of me.

It smelled like old dust, like sorrow and grief. Just when I was about to open it, my grandmother appeared at the end of the stairs. She punished me by making me clean the floors for half of the day. We didn't speak. Yet I know that trunk must have been precious to her… and painful. I truly felt sorry, but there was no way my grandmother would hear anything I had to say. I was a bad girl for stirring up old, locked up memories.

All those memories came flooding in. Just as I was standing in front of the chapel entrance, I could feel the draught piercing my clothes. I was almost waiting for my grandmother to come and scold me for prying where I had no business to be.

"Why am I here?" I asked myself, scrutinizing the interior walls. There was nothing to see other than tags and debris, yet I was mesmerized by the light coming through the windows and by the specks of dust playing in the gentle breeze.

"What can I contribute here?" I closed my eyes. I asked myself to relax while I was holding on to the metal bars and resting my forehead on them.

My head was still looking answers. I took a few deep breaths and I started asking out loud: "What am I aware of?" My dog started to bark as if someone was approaching. I opened my eyes for a few moments listening intently. There was no one. I closed my eyes again. "It must have been a rabbit," I concluded.

My focus softened. It was just an illusion, subtle and surreal. I perceived something that I could describe as an undefined cloud of presences. They were quiet and humble, almost excusing themselves for interrupting my moment of silence. There were a lot of them.

"Can I do something for you?" I asked out loud. "Who are you? Would you like to stay? Or maybe leave? Or is there anything you would like to tell me or anyone else?

The awareness came quick, fast, and sharp: do a clearing. My shoulders relaxed; my breath deepened.

It didn't take long before they disappeared leaving a

sense of calm behind.

I stood in front of the gate for a few more moments receiving the gratitude for having contributed and for acknowledging my entity awareness.

I left the chapel port feeling light and happy.

When I looked back I could tell the building was happy too. There was this peaceful energy to it as if the walls themselves had relaxed.

I took my dog and walked into the forest.

We ventured on a different path, unknown, avid for more adventure.

I was still rewinding the episode in my head when my eyes rested on something shiny among the fallen leaves.

I picked up the object. It was a glittery star pin with the words 'I love you' written on it.

"I love you too!" I shouted. "Thank you for the gift!"

A Gift from Earth

It had been a particularly challenging day.

Days and nights had been following each other without clear and set delineations. I was continuously slaloming between classes, creation meetings, translations (I translate classes from English into Romanian), house, family, animals, daily errands, coffees, and very little sleep.

I was beginning to feel stressed out, but I was telling myself that it was 'positive stress'. To tell the truth, I was dependent on the adrenaline kicks each class ignited in me, after which, it took countless hours to settle down before I could switch activities.

I had been translating night classes that were happening in real time in Australia, which just happens to be the middle of the night my time in Brussels. Doing this has an immense impact on my brain and my body.

I remember getting out on my terrace in the middle of an early morning with a coffee in hand and feeling overwhelmed, yet in a surprisingly delightful way. I was bare foot and almost naked. The cold breeze caused my hairs to rise up and my whole body to quiver in a wake up movement. Even though I wasn't willing to admit it to myself, I was tired. But, there really wasn't any space to whine or complain. I had committed to being present during the class and to deliver. My body, however, was pushing through, demanding more rest.

I took a deep breath and I asked my body what contribution I could be for it.

"Body, what contribution can we be for the Earth? What contribution can we be today for the Earth that would ease this tension right away?" There was no answer; there was just this warmth swirling through my frozen feet in delicate waves. The shivering and the goose bumps were replaced by a rising heat that appeared to turn on all those places of my body where I previously felt depleted. Soon all I could be present with was this incandescent sensation in my body, pulsating with the rhythm of the Earth. My heart rate slowed down. My body started a movement of its own as if part of a cosmic soothing dance. I closed my eyes and allowed the rays of the morning to tickle the top of my nose.

There was this majestic sensation about the start of the day with the sun up on the horizon. The birds started chirping; my neighbours were drawing their curtains; I could hear cars in the distance; and… my heart beating.

I sat down for a moment and soaked all this in. I was still with my feet on the frozen grass. I wasn't cold. I was hot and steaming filled up with the life orgasm. Completely vulnerable, left at the mercy of the powers of the Earth, I could have been smashed in a heartbeat if the Earth desired. Yet, she was so generously welcoming me to satiate my thirst on the nourishing energies until I was ready to move on.

I must have been outside for a while when I abruptly opened my eyes. I knew it was time to get back inside. The class was starting again.

When I finally reached my bed around 9am, I had a huge smile on my face for having received the generosity of the Earth, so caring and so abundant.

I fell asleep dreaming about my garden and all the unseen creatures that make it grow, the way it is for them to enjoy a home, and for us to be nourished by the sight.

I woke up 5 hours later, sharp and refreshed. My dog was waiting for me to come down the stairs and cuddle, as we do every morning. She was particularly restless. We were past her walking time and she was urging me to get going.

We had been spending the past few months having a long walk each day in our magic forest, enjoying the silence and the absence of people. We both loved to not be bothered and just be. It was such a privilege of the Corona times to actually not see anyone around and be the queen of the park.

Though we know this forest by heart, every time we meet Mr. Branch – the handsome tree at the 'gates' of the forest, it's like we step into a magic realm. Time has no relevance and our bodies are tickled with the joy of discovering something new every time. The forest is never the same. It dares to change on us and we are thrilled to explore what else is to be found in this special place.

We walked up to the chapel and from the top of the hill we looked down onto the lawn. It was a breath taking view. I took my shoes off and I started walking on the frozen dead leaves. The temperature shock sent shivers up my spine and made me laugh. I took a deep breath and I simply asked… "Forest, Earth, what can I contribute to you?" I closed my eyes. The message was clear: receive.

I opened my camera and shared these moments with the world on video talking about acknowledging the gift that we all are for the Earth when we allow ourselves to receive its gift. I spoke of how gifting and receiving go hand in hand. How happy are we when we know someone is happy with a gift we so carefully prepared for that person? How much do we receive joy and gift joy? What if the greatest gift we can ever be to the Earth is our lightness, our laughter? After all, laughter heals the Earth while worries wound it.

I was stepping slowly, showing my feet to the camera when something bright got my attention. Deep in the grass, there was a coin shining with droplets of cold mist covering it, glimmering in the sun. I picked it up with the amazement and happiness of a child. That was a miracle! A few steps later, another coin appeared from the grass leaves! And another one! I was laughing my heart out acknowledging that I was gifted the laughter, the healing, the awareness, and the money!

I also noticed that after having found 3 coins, I had decided it was impossible to find another one. And so it was. Later on, replaying the video at home, I noticed a few more coins lying at my feet that I did not see when I was there. "Did I shut the door to receiving more?" I wonder. Who knows? Thank you, entities, for this amazing awareness!

The Old Woman with Milky Blue Eyes

I almost never cook, yet, one evening I had this urge to create a new dish. I invented it from the ingredients I had on hand, and I was surprised how delicious it turned out to be.

I was standing by the kitchen counter dicing an onion so that I could stir fry the base of my dish. I realized I was hungry. Often times when I have these adventures in the kitchen, I discover that it feels like I would die if I didn't eat. I have come to know that whenever I feel this way, there is more to it than just the sudden craving for food.

Stories of the Unseen

I closed my eyes and I asked, "Hmm, who wants to eat? Body, do you want to eat? Is someone else willing to eat? Someone or something? With a body or without a body?" After asking this, I often find that just drinking a glass of water works miracles. Other times interesting food tastes, smells, and pictures are downloaded in my Universe. This time, I became sad, and a clear image of an old woman's face was downloaded into my awareness. Sadness transformed into kindness. It was almost like feeling pity for her. I was fascinated by the detail I received of her face. She had milky blue eyes, red at the interior corner of the eye, and I could see every wrinkle on her face. I could tell she had been crying. She seemed lost and afraid.

"Oh, hello," I said like almost talking to myself.

She seemed to hear me although she kept crying.

"Can I do something for you, granny?" I asked.

The information came from out of nowhere. She died of Covid. She missed her grandchildren. She continued sobbing.

I continued. "Do you know that you died? Do you know that you don't have a body any longer?"

She seemed confused. There was no way for me to make her stay present in the conversation. I noticed she was struggling to breathe as well, and this made her even more agitated. I realized she had been heavily medicated before she died, so it was like talking to someone on drugs. I asked for all the medication in her system to be released and dissipated and I promised her we would talk again, when she was calm and clear. I supposed it would take some time.

When I woke up in the middle of the night, I knew that I hadn't kept my promise. I kind of felt bad about that, not necessarily because someone might have considered me unreliable – after all I gave my word – but because my lack of presence had led to yet another tormented night.

It was 2am and I knew she was back. With my nose on my pillow, I told myself that this was the beginner's mistake. I promised I would talk to her; I just didn't tell her on what terms and conditions.

She only came back to thank me. That was all. The sadness was gone. The confusion was dissipated. She left as fast as she arrived.

I turned on my side and continued sleeping, grateful for the gift of the tools I had to deal with the entities, because they work no matter the moment in time, lifetime, or dimension.

Asking for a Miracle

It's a fresh crisp October day. I wake up with a lazy stretch of my whole body. The sun is tickling my nose. Today is a very special day! It's my husband's birthday. I touch my bum and scratch it gently. I'm pregnant with our third child. He happened unexpectedly yet… I knew exactly when it happened.

I slide out of the sheets with the expectation of a gorgeous day! The smell of freshly brewed coffee invites reverie into my morning. It's going to be a full day. My husband hugs me and kisses me on my forehead.

"Happy birthday!" I say to him.

He mumbles in response. In contrast with my enthusiasm, he's not quite willing to take a day off from work, not even on his birthday. He had already brought the other two kids to school and to the nanny. We will have half a day to ourselves.

"Are you excited?" I ask while I stuff myself with some red fleshy strawberries. "How many houses are we going to visit? 3? I can hardly wait!"

If it were up to me, I would book visits of houses just to see how other people live. It's so thrilling to get into someone's house that you don't know and to figure out who they are, and what's important to them. I find it fabulous!

Licking the chocolate from my fingers, I added, "This is the best breakfast: strawberries and chocolate by the spoon."

One hour later we are already on our house hunting tour. The agent is waiting for us by the first address, just a bit further down our street. We stop in front of the entrance and look at the 2 doors in front of us with me inquiring which one should be the one to take. The agent opens both of them. One opens into an office or private practice, the other one opens into a long corridor leading to the main part of the house and to the stairs that would lead up to what the agent calls a rented apartment.

Besides the surprise of the architecture of this house, with no window in the living room yet plenty of light coming from the glass ceiling, there is this huge space, different from anything we have seen before. We walk through the house with curiosity. The previous owner had left it half-finished. He had enough of the expenses the house swallowed in renovation. He was in a difficult financial position and needed to sell the house as fast as possible.

The autumn rays of a cold sun are reaching us from the terrace. I slide the terrace door open and I scream with excitement. A huge elevated terrace is marking the borders of a wild grown garden. I run down the few steps and I look at the house from the back with my feet playing in the fallen leaves. I picture the kids playing in the garden, having fun on sunny Sundays. I know that this is going to be our house, even though it is way out of our budget.

The agent says it's time to visit the second house. Just before leaving I take a moment:

"Hello beautiful, would you like us to come and live here? I would love to be here. The baby would too. Let's make a deal. If you want us here, please help us get a price that we can afford. If not, no hard feelings. You are beautiful and anybody would be happy to be protected by you."

The house hunting tour continues. We view more houses. I know that the first house is calling and pulling us to live there. I look at my husband. He doesn't seem too excited. I am not sure whether this is a trick or maybe he is concerned about the price.

I can tell it's lunchtime, because my stomach starts making strange noises. We head to the centre of the city to look for a nice place to eat.

"Which house did you like most?" I ask him while munching on the nuts that came as a side serving to his beer.

"I am not sure," he replied confused. "They are all so different, and is it my imagination or did they have different energies to them? I mean the one by the forest was beautiful, but I had the feeling that someone was going to break in at any moment. The owners also seemed concerned by this. And the other one, the artist's one… Well, it's funny how people don't realize how strangers perceive their world. I mean… all those empty bottles on the floor... and the ashtrays… That sight didn't make me try to imagine myself in it. The first one though… I like it, but we cannot afford it." He looked at me with saddened eyes. "I know it's your favourite, but…" he continued, "As I look at it today, we need a miracle to be able to pay for it."

"I know. There is something about the first house that made me picture myself in it. It likes us. Who knows, maybe the miracle is not coming from where we expect it." We then change the subject of the conversation. What is going to be for dinner? Who will pick up the children from school?

Later in the afternoon when the kids are at home, there's an excitement in the air that words cannot describe. I am laughing and giggling as if I know something extraordinary is about to happen.

Between splashes of soap bubbles in the bathroom and preparing dinner, I miss the phone ringing. It's evening by now.

We sit down. We feed the kids in turn and when they are finally in bed, we pop a bottle of champagne and cuddle on the couch to watch the news from the French broadcast.

"The agent called back," my husband starts in a hesitant voice. "It's about the first house. The owner insisted on his price and I made an offer myself. It's a shameless way lower offer. But hey, we've got nothing to lose, right?"

"And?" I am waiting impatiently for the continuation.

"It's ours! I would have never thought I could pull this off. Except that it worked. We will sign the agreement on Monday!"

"Cheers to our new home! Double trouble on your birthday, Mister!"

***

Months later we are ready to move in. I'm 8.5 months pregnant and I have not visited the house since. We didn't receive the keys until all documents were signed and the house was insured.

We cross the threshold holding our breaths. Once inside my spine is hit by a current of cold air. My head starts spinning; my heart starts racing. "What's going on?" I ask leaning towards one of the corridor walls? There's this sadness and heaviness on my shoulders coming from nowhere. The walls seem cold. The house seems unwelcoming, as if all the magic I saw in it during our visit had vanished. I am confused. I am angry.

I don't get it. I sit down and sob. This is it? It doesn't

look anything like what we saw the first time. I am so disappointed. "You wanted us here, didn't you?" I asked the house touching one of the walls. "What happened to you?" The long corridor looks frightening. The stairs seem dangerously steep and slippery.

My ears keep buzzing and making me dizzy. I rush towards the terrace to get a breath of fresh air. I slide the terrace door open. The fresh spring breeze caresses my cheeks.

Just in front of me there is this majestic wild cherry tree in full bloom. It is breathtakingly beautiful, as if straight from the Japanese Sakura. It is waving to me an abundant welcome to the new house. White delicate petals shiver in the wind, a snowfall of flowers. The dried leaves are engulfed by the bold and brave grass pointing out from the ground in the garden.

I call my husband outside. We look speechless at the tree.

"Did you see the tree when we came to visit? I can't remember any tree in this garden." I continued searching in the distance. Wild bamboo was dancing in the spring breeze from the end of the garden and…

"Can you smell this?" I ask him. "It smells like… lilac!"

There it is, in bloom, exposing its scented joy buds. The lilac tree greets us with an explosion of dark purple flowers.

"I always received lilac branches from my best friend in Romania on my birthday. Now I'll have a tree all for myself!" I jumped with joy holding my belly laughing.

It all came together: I had asked the house for a miracle. I trusted it, but I had never acknowledged that I received what I had asked for.

"Thank you sweet house for all these miracles you've been offering us. Thank you for the welcome presents. Your garden is magic. I wish for you to be happy with us here, as we surely are delighted with you. Could you please contribute for a smooth move in?"

The sorrow, the tears, and the despair disappeared completely. Sometimes all you have to do is acknowledge that you received what you had asked for.

Our third son was born the day the final works in the house were ready. A miracle! Yes, another miracle!

The Cherry Tree

There's an empty chair under my cherry tree in bloom.

I smile. Whenever my mom used to visit us, although she had never witnessed the cherry tree in bloom, she would ask one of us to put a chair under the tree for her. She could not see much, yet she seemed to have this bond with our garden. She would sit silent on the chair while the tumult of our family life with small children was following its hectic course. I knew that she had a hard time fitting into our way of raising the children with our irregular meal times and questioning and adjusting each and every day to what would function the best for us.

It often hurt her to see me take the first place in my family and being bold about what worked for me. She had put her whole life in last place, making sure everybody was happy, before she could sink in a chair and sip a coffee in peace.

I remember all those instances when I would panic if I didn't know exactly where she was. I was mothering her and she just didn't want to be the kid. She had been the strongest woman I had ever known in my life and the safest fortress for any emotion or feeling she might have had towards her children. She would never complain, and she would always do things secretly so that she didn't bother people for 'nothings' as she called them. As long as she could do stuff by herself, she would never ask for support - a lesson that I learned from her and for which I paid with my joy.

Even though she died years ago, by some strange coincidence, from time to time there's an empty chair under the cherry tree. She sits quietly taking in the beauty of her tree, which is getting more and more beautiful with every year that passes by.

I ignored her presence. I cursed her presence. I denied her presence. I rejected and refused her presence. Yet… I know she is there. She doesn't come for me. She is here for the kids. She was always head over heels for the kids.

She had died on Christmas night. I used all my resources of shifting the pain into a silver lining so that I would not have to face the anger at her dying. It was unfair. This was all I could think of. It was brutal and unkind to be willing to leave this world on such a day of celebration. Until very recently, I couldn't get over this somehow treacherous departing. Truth be told… it wasn't a surprise. The real surprise was to acknowledge that we both knew she would die, but at the time none of us knew exactly what we were aware of.

Once the pain faded with the years, I was finally willing to look at her death with different eyes. There must have been something else underneath her cold appearance. Those blue eyes of hers were sparkling with so much love of life, which dimmed when she lost her eyesight. She died almost blind.

Knowing what I know today, this has been a healing journey not only for myself but for her as well.

It was during an intuition workshop that I got a glimpse of what I was aware of and the sharpness of my awareness. There was this particular exercise where we had to sit in a circle and write some names on pieces of paper, of alive persons and deceased ones. We folded the pieces of paper, and mixed them in a bowl. Then, one by one, we each picked a piece of paper from the bowl. Just through connecting to the energy of what was written on the small note, we would guess if it was an embodied entity or a disembodied one. Could it be described as feminine or masculine? What else could we say about what was playing in between our hands and the energetic awareness of the entities playing with us?

Up to this point, I didn't quite like the idea to talk about dead people and I was freaking out just by listening to the accuracy of what the others were describing. I was convinced that I would just fail miserably.

My turn came to pick out a note. I held it in my hands, kind of praying to not be ridiculed on the way. My cheeks became hot. My body became excited. I started to laugh.

"Well, I can tell you that this person used to laugh a lot. There's such a light, bubbly easy energy about her… It's a she. It's definitely a female presence. My hands started to tremor. I took a deep breath fighting my tears. She is dead. The words resonated in my head like a gong reverberating in my whole body. And her name is Maria. She is my mother."

There was this awkward silence that followed.

I opened the note and my tears flooded the little piece of yellow paper: my mother.

All I could think of was… how was it possible to miss this liveliness of hers when she was still here? All I could remember of her were a few jokes here and there and a lot of pain and sadness by the end of her life. I had a lot of concern and feared interaction with her. She was blind, had heart problems, was severely diabetic, and suffered from Parkinson's and psoriasis which shamed her more than anything else. She also was on a lot of medications.

I took a few more minutes to take this experience in before I looked around me. Apparently her presence was so powerful that it didn't leave anyone untouched. Yet, my heart was still hurting.

Later the same evening, lingering around a glass of wine, I acknowledged to myself that this kindness, caring, this lightness of spirit and this joy of life had not been unknown to me. Even when we reached her apartment after she died, the whole space was filled with her spirit. There were our favourite cookies on a platter, our favourite foods filling the fridge, the Christmas tree, and the joy of the winter celebrations. She enjoyed us being there… as she watched from the skies.

The day after the funeral I overslept and I completely missed a remembering mass because of the time difference between Belgium and Romania. When I reached the church and I realized what had happened, I burst out laughing to the unhappy surprise of my uncle who considered my behaviour outrageous. Yet… I knew my mom didn't mind. She was at peace.

However, from time to time I would be enraged with her dying like that. And then, like a reminder, an empty chair would be left under the cherry tree. And my heart would soften and I would allow myself to sob, missing her, and allow myself to be missed by her.

What a gift to know that she chooses over and over to be here with us, until the day when she will no longer choose this. Then, I would be honoured to be there for her to facilitate her step towards a different reality.

Beings of Light

I recently chose to follow some dance routines on YouTube. Nothing fancy yet something that would allow my body to get back in motion and regain a sense of being alive and free. If there is something I am proud I inherited from my mom, it's a certain flexibility in my muscles and joints, which used to be admired by people who were suffering of stiffness.

It's been four years since I have done any physical activity. I stopped after I tortured my body by doing a 20km race across Brussels. I did it to prove to myself I could. I had been battling my extra weight my whole life. I even had a bariatric surgery and nothing seemed to work - not even a strict diet and training four times a week.

I ran that race; I crossed the finish line, and then… nothing. I drank a bottle of champagne and I never wanted to run or jog again. Though my quest didn't leave visible traumas on my body, I became aware of a resistance to anything and anyone who would suggest a new way of eating or exercising.

There's a time for all and everything. My time had come to re-appropriate my body. I had signed up to a program with a different perspective on eating. The best that could happen was to lose a few kilograms; the worst thing that could happen was to get expensively educated on food, nutrition, and fixed points of view on following a strict diet.

There I was, lying breathless on the floor. I was flat on my back, hands and legs spread, searching for the position that would offer the maximum tension release from my body. It had been a particularly daring choreography especially when my competitive warrior side kicked in.

It was so common for me to push myself to the limit without a frown on my face. Today, letting go of the need to push myself over the limits proved to be a challenge. Yet, at some point there was this voice whispering in my ear that all was well. I didn't have to go the extra mile. I could just enjoy and feel the sensations in my body.

While jumping and turning and squatting, my joints started to hurt. Sweat was wetting my t-shirt abundantly and I knew I was reaching the end of my resources. There's always more, and better; and there's also the willingness to let go of the struggle, as familiar as it might be, and relax.

I rolled to one side breathing deeply. There were 1001 thoughts racing in my head. It was as if they were waiting for me to calm down so that they could assault me. I closed my eyes and I expanded my being way outside my body. I perceived it like a golden fluid gel flowing in all directions at the same time. First, I filled up the room, the whole house, then spread it across the city, the country, and the continent. I kept breathing and expanding.

There was so much peace in my world. There was nothing to be done, to be thought, or to be emotional about. There was just a deep perception of space and quietness. Tears started welling up under my lids.

I called in my team mates. I never had a thought about them before and right at that moment it seemed obvious that I would summon them. I asked them to touch my body and to teach me what receiving from them meant. I perceived a soft pressure at the base of my neck at the back and a distinct sensation of floating. Then, my head was racing again. Was it panic? Was it fear? "Shut up!" I urged the voices to silence. I lowered all the barriers and protections and I allowed myself to be.

It started to be very warm in the room, yet my feet were freezing. My cheeks were on fire. They felt as if someone was caressing them gently. Shortly after, my forehead became hot. It wasn't unpleasant, just different. I kept my eyes closed at the same perceiving this dancing light above me, like a soft soothing cushion of healing. I had this clear impression that there was so much peace and calm, kindness and love in this touch.

My tears were rolling down my cheeks and soon I was sobbing uncontrollably. It was like I was enveloped in a soft velvety cocoon of gratitude. It was immense, flowing through all my cells and molecules of my body. I had this distinct impression that thousands and thousands of invisible hands were tickling my body, reviving it, filling it with glowing sparkles. I let it happen.

And then I didn't. I have no idea how long I was lying on the carpet. When I finally stood up I knew that my request was granted. I had asked for my team mates to come and they brought the Beings of Light[3] to me to show me what receiving from entities truly was. There was no ritual to be done; no words to be said; simply the willingness to let go of the shields that one wears all the time. It was an act of courage, of vulnerability, and of nakedness in the face of the invisible. It also was an act of trust in what I know, and gratitude for who I truly be.

"I am deeply humbled and honoured. Thank you."

Golden Wings

I love jewellery. I adore gold.

Actually, one of my favourite ways of spending some time by myself is to take out my jewellery – costume or gold – look at it, clean it, play with it, talk to it, and check from time to time if we are still in a loving relationship. Like with any other relationship, emotions sometimes run flat, you find the enthusiasm is no longer there, and maybe it is time to move on and ask for an upgrade.

For a long time I behaved like some sort of a Gollum seeing my bijoux, my jewels, as my precious. I would hurt like crazy when I would discover that some piece was missing, going directly to "Someone stole my ring!" instead of allowing myself to know that we went separate ways. I knew exactly when my awareness was correct, and also when I didn't want to admit that maybe the attraction factor between me and a certain piece had diminished.

It is not uncommon for me to wear my favourite jewellery, a drop of perfume, and drink a cup of coffee naked on my sunny terrace. It's a moment of pure and almost selfish hedonism that reconnects me to the joyful essence of my body. We don't need much to be happy. Maybe a bit of gold, a diamond or two, a sparkling stone, some creamy pearls…

My husband knows by now. If there is something that makes me happy, it is a piece of crafted gold that fits me like a fluid glove. And when he says 'no' I am ready for battle because nothing and no one will stand between me and what I desire. It is also exciting to look at myself and see what inventive ways I can come up with to get what I lust after.

It was during one trip to Costa Rica that we almost divorced over a pair of earrings.

***

It's hot; so hot that I'm likely to sweat my brains out. Clothes are sticking to my body right after coming out of the shower. I'm getting ready for an Antique Guild[1] show just before dinner. It's one of the events I have been impatiently waiting for. It's the only occasion that I know of where I am allowed to try on all sorts of exquisite, gorgeous bejewelled beauties, and have a feel of what being plunged in a world of richness contributes to my life.

I have already decided that there are pieces I cannot afford. I laugh at myself. Is there truly anything that I cannot afford, or is it just that I haven't chosen to possess those things? Not everything is appealing to my eye, not everything sublimates my body. And we both know – my body and I – that we cannot force either of us into a choice that is not working, because at the end of the day, we pay the final 'bill' which mostly is an energetic one.

Have you ever tried to wear something that your body doesn't like? It will do everything possible to make you get rid of it. I have foolishly made the choice to wear things my body wasn't fond of for many reasons like…I paid a fortune for it, it should fit, I'd better make it work…"What if I asked a question?" I say to myself while closing the door of the bungalow behind me on my way to the event.

The venue is generously lit up in the dark night. Pieces of exquisite jewellery are shining inviting us to touch them and try them on. There's beauty and luxury and a sense of everything being possible.

I am annoyed by the heat. Drops of salty water appear above my lip giving me a touchy sensation. I walk round the main tables watching the bodies enjoy the precious brushes of gold and platinum on the aroused skin. It's delicious and delightful.

There is nothing that pings me. None of the pieces are talking to me. They seem busy with other clients somehow knowing that we are 'not a match'. I ask for a glass of champagne from the bar and take the view in. I take time to observe the people. There's so much wealth in front of me, and I am part of it. I take a sip and enjoy the bubbles awakening my tongue and my palate.

"Can you help me with this?" One of my friends presents me the back of her neck to release her hair from the clutch of a stunning gold necklace. I know she is going to sleep with it tonight and I smile.

"What do you think?" she turns around proud of her finding.

"I don't!" We both laugh at our joke. "I prefer not to think. Ask your body? Yet I'm pretty sure that you have your answer! Cheers to that!" She kisses me on the cheek and melts into the crowd.

I leave the bar corner and have a new look at what has been left on the tables. Sometimes people fall in love with some pieces, they try them on, then they decide something else is much more appealing. Who knows, maybe I'll find something for me.

"Oh, excuse me!" I apologize for having bumped unintentionally against one of the ladies close to the display.

"No, no worries, I was just leaving. You can take my spot if you'd like."

I advance towards the mirror in front of me noticing my eyes and my smile. My body is enjoying the other excited bodies. I randomly touch a few of the rings. I observe a subtle change in the taste of my mouth at the same time. A see a hand coming from above me, from the back, dropping something just in front of me: a pair of earrings in the shape of wings, accentuated by a dark stone. They are smooth and glossy, gliding under my thumb, launching almost a sexual feeling to the touch. I moan.

I pick both of them up and position my body in front of the mirror. I try them on and I transform in front of my eyes. Some people witness the moment. My hair is done with tsarina-like braids tonight. The addition of the earrings to this look has a special effect on me. I sigh.

"Will you make me money if I buy you?" I asked them while holding them close to my solar plexus.

"No."

That's strange! Then what's this excitement that I'm feeling?

"Will you expand my world?"

"Yes!"

"OK, then let's make a deal. You are mine but you'll have to make sure nobody touches you until I get the money."

I ask for them to be set aside until the payment is completed.

Later in the night, I sit on my bed sobbing about the earrings. My husband didn't like the idea of investing that money in a pair of earrings. He didn't agree to finance me and my "outrageous" idea. My funds were running out, my credit card was maxed, and all I knew was that even if it cost me a divorce, I would not leave without those earrings.

I tossed and turned for a whole night when suddenly I found the solution.

I asked my husband for a loan. I would pay it back in six months. The next morning, the payment was done just before we packed for returning home. The earrings came to me in a deep blue velvet pouch. They were looking for me in the conference room. When we met I knew we were in for a ride.

I put them on and soaked in the precious energies they were bringing into my life. They truly represented a financial stretch and upgrade, and also caused the stir of a lot of unsaid points of view. They urged me to be present, to ask, to demand, and to request what I really desired to create as a future in my life, starting with the way I was communicating about money with my husband and the structures we had put in place so that we don't get close to what was uncomfortable. Touché!

***

My ears hurt. They are red and swollen and my ear lobes are throbbing. It crosses my mind that I hadn't sanitized my earrings before wearing them. I dismiss the thought. I'll take them off when we land in about 10 hours.

Touchdown. I can hardly open my eyes. My head hurts as if I had been drinking the whole night. I make a note in my head to not have alcoholic drinks while flying. I must be dehydrated. I accidentally touch my ears while stretching. They are festering from under the earrings. "That's interesting…"

Once home, I remove them and clean them. My ears look like red slices of watermelon. "Am I allergic to my earrings? Now that's an expensive allergy," I joke.

Within 2 weeks my ears have recovered. Time to show off my new jewellery in a workshop I am organizing. My head starts to hurt. It feels like someone is poking my eyes out with hundreds of thin needles. I choose to change my outfit into something more colourful. I change my earrings as well. The discomfort vanishes as if by magic.

"Maybe I should just admit that I made a bad investment," I am soothing myself holding the gold wing earrings with the diamond cut sapphires in my hand. "How could I have been so wrong, though?"

I rewind the whole story in my mind.

"But, of course!" I shout with excitement. "I told you to not let anyone touch you! Anyone includes me, smarty pants! Thank you for having done such a marvellous job, sweet earrings! Can we now fire all the entities that we asked to guard you and will you please be the joy I know you truly are?"

***

In case you're wondering, my ears never hurt again after that moment. Those earrings are still my favourite ones of my whole collection. And yes, they keep expanding my world every time I invite them to bring in the energies of greatness.

PS. I did pay the loan from my husband… in only 3 months… as if by magic!

Birthday Wish

In 2019, I chose to spend my birthday in Langkawi, Malaysia, by the ocean. I am at an Access Consciousness event with lots of other people and I am one of the lucky ones who doesn't have to share a room. The view of the ocean behind rich coconut trees spoils my eyes with beauty. The sound of the waves gently crashing on the soft white sand of the shore is soothing for my body. The breeze flows minuscule molecules of salt on my lips. There's so much joy here…

The sign on the balcony warns me not to leave the window open. Monkeys are known to steal personal things from the rooms, sometimes never to be found again. It find it hilarious, yet I am sure the victims of monkey theft wouldn't find it funny at all.

I arrived a day ago and I haven't yet been down to the beach. I don't have words to describe why other than apprehension.

I adore water and my body adores the freedom of movement and the joyful lack of gravity while in it. Yet, I have this deep fear of it. I don't have a cognitive explanation other than the conclusion that I must have drowned during some other lifetime and somehow my body remembers the experience.

***

A few years previously I tried to get over my fear. I took a guided diving lesson in the Maldives, in the friendly turquoise waters of Kani Island. It seemed a fun idea until… it wasn't. The instructor was teaching me how to put on and remove my mask with simple precise gestures. We did the drill together for a few times until he trusted me enough to have a first dive.

We did some exercises at the surface to begin. The sequence of movements was simple and precise. Then we went 1 metre deep. Then 1.5 metres. I was supposed to follow his underwater instructions closely and not come out in one launch under any circumstances. He had warned me that my brain would tell me to remove the mask to get more oxygen, and that I had to trick it into breathing through the mouth and not the nose.

He gave me the thumbs up and urged me to look at his diving mask when I started the exercise. I panicked. The next thing I knew is that I was breathing turquoise salty water through my nose. I launched out of the water hardly containing my tears. There was no way I would go dive again.

He called in his assistant diver, Yuki, a former competition diver from Japan. She coached me into agreeing to have another go. Her motto was: "The ocean is your friend. Treat it with respect. You would not like to leave your friend's house and leave him with the impression that you are upset with each other. Your friend deserves a heartfelt good-bye, if this is your wish."

She knew how to talk to me and she got me under water. Second attempt. Second failure. I jumped out of the water gasping for air like a dying fish on the beach. By this time I was judging myself beyond any possible pleasure or connection with the element of water. I was done.

"I get it," she said softly, appearing out of nowhere

next to me. "Diving might not be for everyone, and it's not wrong. But would you allow me to show you something fascinating? No more exercises, I promise. Just hold the guide wire under water and advance at your own pace. I am next to you."

We dove again. I was advancing cautiously deeper and deeper in the water holding onto the iron wire attached to floating pegs. Small coloured fish appeared from nowhere swirling in front of my eyes. Corals. Algae. We were now 3 metres deep. My eyes were taking it all in. I smiled and looked for Yuki. She was right next to me nodding. My mask was now filled with tears of gratitude for the beauty that opened up in front of my eyes when I chose to get over my fear and to trust my body's love of water. I also had this exceptional trainer next to me.

My diving teacher approached me making a sign that I had to go back to the surface. Slowly, flapping my diving fins, taking my time, enjoying the weightless movements even with 20 kg of gear on my back, I stepped out of the water knowing that "the ocean is my friend."

***

As I sit remembering this moment, I realize it is time for lunch. Maybe I will go to the beach and enjoy a cocktail in the shade of one of the draped lounges in the sand.

I took the sinuous path to the beach bar alongside the hotel building. A wooden walkway was guiding my steps out of the heated sand. My eyes caught the notice board: "In case of Tsunami alert…" I froze, incapable of advancing. I decided this ideal ocean view revealing itself in front of my eyes was a deadly one. My mood changed. I became melancholic and sad, and I suddenly missed my family.

I ordered a gin & tonic and lay on one of the puffy chairs sheltered by thin veil curtains waving in the wind. I was thoughtless yet fully aware of the energies flowing through me: wonder, apprehension, curiosity, nurturance, care, gratitude, sadness, despair, ignorance, wind, water, living organism, heat, refreshing breath, and my body responding to all of them.

The day goes on and now I am enjoying a delightful dinner at the beach. It is a celebration of us all there kicking off a 7-day event in an idyllic place, secluded from the rest of the world, yet in communion with all the elements around us. We were all asking for more consciousness for both us and Planet Earth, regardless of how that showed up for each of us. I loved seeing all my friends together having a good time and laughing. Still, I am aware of the sadness that I cannot shake off.

"What is this?" I whisper.

I peer down at the blackness of the ocean. Mighty, powerful, unwelcoming, unforgiving… source of life on Planet Earth, invaluable resource of knowledge and awareness. The significance weighs me down. I stand up from the table and I excuse myself for the night. I walk down to the beach on the way to my room. There's no other light except that from the party tent on the beach by the bar.

When I am far enough away, I take my dress off and walk naked in the water. I am scared, yet I know the ocean is my friend. "What can I contribute to you, Lady of the Night?" I sink my whole body into the water facing the sea. Small tickling waves rock my body gently. I am not alone. I might be the only undressed body in the water, but I am not alone. My skin contracts. There's no wind, yet I perceive a cold draught in the water.

"What can I be for you?"

A surge of sadness and unease reminded me of the

sign about the tsunami by the beach.

A few years back there had been a tsunami in nearby Thailand that was caused by a huge earthquake in the Indian Ocean. Over 200 000 people had died. I closed my eyes and I allowed the restlessness in my body to wear off. All of a sudden, I became aware of the sadness, the fear, and the anger of those who died. They seemed stuck between worlds, as if suspended in a 3D picture. Some are still lingering on the waves, lost, never reaching the shores.

I spoke to them. "Would any of you like to leave and make a different choice? Is now the time?" I asked out loud.

I closed my eyes and allowed the clearing tools to work their magic. The fear disappeared; the sadness was gone. "Thank you for receiving my contribution!" I exclaimed. I was joyful, happy, and so looking forward to my birthday the next day.

***

It's my birthday! The sun is already up in the sky. I grab my phone to check the time. 6:45 am. I jump out of my bed with the exuberance of a child ready for the biggest adventure of her life. I put on the dress that I had chosen for my celebration day, and lavish myself in a ray of perfume. I wear gold lipstick and… no underwear! I am so excited, and every minute spent in the room seems like a wasted chance for miracles.

I fly down the stairs and run barefoot to the beach holding on to my long dress. I giggle; I laugh; I am so alive! I walk straight to the water and allow it to play around my ankles. The sensation arouses all the molecules in my body. My hair escapes its loose bun and waves playfully in the sun.

"Good morning, Lady Ocean!" I shouted out. "Today is my birthday! On birthdays we have a wish granted, right?" Nobody was answering and I didn't want to take the chance of hearing a "no" coming out of my head. "Therefore, my wish is…" I take a deep breath. "Will you please show me what communion is for me? Will you also show me what I know about the elementals that I have not yet acknowledged? That's it! Can I have the magic now, please?"

I lift my dress and I turn around a few times like little girls adorned in fancy dresses do, and I drop myself on the beach. The warm grains of sand on my butt make me burst out laughing. I feel high on joy and happiness! I have no idea how long I have kept my eyes shut tightly wishing for my dream to come true when I heard someone shout, "Dolphins, there, to the right!"

Just in front of me, a few dozen metres from the shore, a family of dolphins were playing in the waters. They were joyful, carefree, springing high above the waters and splashing back into the waves. There was this relaxation and peaceful play, intense and present, and it pulled me in knowing and recognizing for a nanosecond that I am a dolphin myself. The awareness took me by surprise flooding me with a gush of gratitude for it all. I am beyond words, beyond whatever I had decided I am or not in this embodied experience on Earth. And there was also something else…

Tiny, almost imperceptible specks of light were travelling fast in all directions, dancing in front of my eyes as fireflies would dance in an enchanted forest.

"My wish is granted! Thank you!"

I had never seen them before. I had no idea what the elementals could be like, yet I knew they are part of the communion we all have access to with the ALL. You just have to ask.

Malaysian Airlines

"Welcome to Brussels," the voice of the flight attendant resonated in my headphones. She sounds tired, slightly irritated, and relieved to be finally landing. My heart starts racing. My eyes fill with tears.

24 hours earlier…

Langkawi Airport. Our departure for Kuala Lumpur is delayed by 20 minutes. Then, one hour. There is a storm keeping the planes on the ground and the pilots are patiently looking for the weather to calm down. It's the last flight out and any delay means a much higher probability to miss the connecting flight. We are 12 wizards preparing to board this plane.

I find my body is alert and knowing. The restlessness of the other passengers intensifies. I choose to close my eyes, lower the barriers, and expand. Zwooooooosh! My hands open wide and start to dance. I get that I am not only one; my fellow travellers are doing the same. We just finished a spectacular 7-day event where we have been exercising our energetic capacities. Now, we were putting what we learned into practice.

The doors of the waiting room suddenly open and we are invited to walk in the rain to the tarmac. I head to the end rows of the plane with my 2 Belgian travel companions. I realize that the 12 of us are distributed quite evenly on the plane, covering the front, the middle, and the back of it.

I have an aisle seat. On the other side of the aisle sit a few women and their children.

We get clearance for departure. The plane rushes for take-off. And there is this fraction of a second when it skids just before it takes off. And I know.

Looking outside the window, the raindrops whip the plane incessantly. All we can see is a white light pulsating in the darkness and the silhouette of the right wing of the plane. We've only been in the air for five minutes, and we already know that the odds are not looking favourable when the plane makes a sudden move, takes a dive, and shakes from all its joints.

I look at my friends. And I know… without a word, our hands lift up and start reweaving the reality. We call in the elementals; we call in the energies of communion; we open the space for miracles. I perceive a wave of energy rushing through my body from my feet to the top of my head and from the top of my head to my feet. It's like the molecules of my body are no longer mine. They just are.

My mind vanishes. I am somewhere else, beyond the metal frame of a probably crashing airplane. I am beyond, and I am not alone. There's this ball of energy of impossible possibilities fuelled by All. Time stops enough for the plane to receive our contribution and hold it together. We open a space and I send a trickle of light shooting towards my husband at home: I love you. There is a chance we might not make it.

I lift my head as if in a trance. The hallway is filled with entities. I stare in the air and I <u>know</u>. I say, "It's not our time. Would you please contribute to all of us?" I get a "yes" and I am confident. "Thank you!" I whisper. I glance at my friends. They know it too. We've got this. We don't talk. We just be. We are the immensity of magic and miracles on legs. Our hands dance with the energies.

Kids are crying. Moms look at us terrified and reassured at the same time. They see our composed faces and hands caressing the air and they know they are safe. The Universe and its wizards have their backs. They contribute silently.

We land in Kuala Lumpur. Nobody is moving. Passengers sit quietly in their seats as if numb. Like in a slow motion video, people take their time to grab their belongings. We're silent as well.

The arrival hall is unusually quiet. We queue for the border control. One mom touches my hand briefly on the way out. I know and she knows. Moms know. "Thank you," she whispers with tears in her eyes and gratitude. I nod. I don't know what to tell her. She hugs me. I put my hands around her and melt with the immensity of what just happened.

"Have we just saved the plane from crashing?" I wonder, convinced that I am inventing all of it.

I grab my phone to talk to my husband. No network. We rush to catch our connection to Doha. I fall asleep the second I sit in my chair.

**

At the same time in the world: a plane lands on fire in Moscow. Another plane is forced to change routes due to a storm damaging its computer system above the ocean. Connection flights get messed up all over the world.

At the same time at home: my husband wakes up suddenly and opens up the online tracking system of our flight. He sees we are in trouble caught in the storms that have ravaged India for the past few days. He reads 'Malaysian Airlines' and realizes we were in the same type of flight that had crashed a few months earlier. And he knows.

***

"Welcome to Brussels," the voice of the flight attendant resonates in my headphones. She sounds tired, slightly irritated and relieved to be finally landing. My heart starts racing. My eyes fill with tears. I am exploding with gratitude. I am alive. I am aware. I am able.

And I smile. "Thank you, Universe! Now, can I please have more ease with my capacities? What if we didn't need extremes to just be who we are? What if what we always thought to be impossible is possible?"

Sugar High

Brussels rhymes with mussels. To me it is this astonishing composition of smells and flavours and tastes that twirl your senses and lure you into a curious land of "impossible possibles". In other words, Brussels smells like mussels, roasted chicken, fresh fish, car pollution, Starbucks coffee, and Moroccan patisserie next to a 'friet kot'. All senses get confounded.

I used to love my trips to the city center. There were always people in motion, heads filled with thoughts, and a simple way to escape my own life by lingering in busy shops and buying useless things in search of something to fill a void I used to feel inside.

I had a ritual of my own. I would go to the same shops, look at the same kinds of things, and eat at the same places, pretending I was embracing a new lifestyle. I was actually cunningly escaping my awareness and my unwillingness to be present with it.

Shopping was my favourite way to keep myself under control. Clothes shopping, to be more specific. I would go to a shop, eye the clothes, try them on, already knowing I would be disappointed, and tick yet another judgment on my self-destruction list. The clothes would not fit, but they would give me the perfect reason to judge my body!

It recently occurred to me how angry I used to be while shopping. This world doesn't allow you to get angry. It's not done. It's not nice. One should be ashamed of anger and take some anger management classes or support, right? For a long time I didn't ask a question about any of my shopping outbursts. My husband hated my outings as I would drag him to all the shops and torture him to tell me his opinion – which didn't matter by the way. Still, there was this addictive side of the shopping experience that I couldn't let go.

One day, while standing in front of the cashier desk, the lady behind the counter threw a look at me as if assessing whether I was a good or bad client while taking my clothes for scanning. I had just come out of one of the dressing rooms half unhappy with a dress I had tried on. It felt like everybody was looking at me and spying on my moves.

"She has heard my accent. She has figured out I am 'yet another immigrant', and therefore, is treating me disrespectfully," I thought to myself with a subtle, yet, dramatic shake of my head.

Hardly talking to me, the shop assistant literally threw the bag with my clothes towards my side of the counter barking the total price.

"Are you upset?" I asked in a husky tone of voice, handing her my bank card.

"No, why?" she replied instantly, avoiding my eyes.

"Well, you've just thrown the bag at me. Is there something wrong with me?"

"Why would you say that? What are you insinuating?"

She removed herself from behind the case screen and looked me straight in the eyes challenging me in what I knew would be an unsolicited argument.

It took a fraction of a second to rewind my visit in the shop. "What is this all about? What am I aware of? Who am I being here? Who is having this conversation?"

The download was instant. It was a battle of demons and they were not even mine! Great! Party time!

"Thank you!" I said, smiling to her and running the demon clearing[5] in my head. I didn't say anything else. I smiled politely and exited the shop with a fast and steady step. It felt as if I was ending a lifelong war that was not even mine.

"That was fun!" I smile at my husband acknowledging the immense potency of not engaging with demon energies. It was like the skies were deeper than before, and the colours brighter! Even my body was lighter and happier!

"Let's eat something!" I had decreed, already picturing in my mind mountains of ice cream and chocolate topping. All those street smells were making me hungry. So hungry!

"Ice cream is not food," my husband observed.

"Then waffles… something sugary!" I was drooling already.

We didn't have time to sit down and eat. I was craving something quick! We grabbed 2 hot waffles and jumped in the car. We were planning to eat them on the way back home.

"Oh, my goodness, this is heaven! Mhhh, mhhh! This is the best waffle I have ever had!" I kept chewing and talking at the same time, swallowing big chunks of the pastry and licking my fingers from any trace of sugar.

"Who are you?" my husband asked jokingly. "What have you done with my wife?" he continued laughing wickedly.

I suddenly stopped and turned my head to the back seat. There was this density pulling me towards the rear seats of the car.

"Is this marijuana?" I asked, sniffing the scent in the air. "Where…?"

Our car had been left at the underground level of an old public parking garage. It had a creepy look, but it was the only parking accessible at the time. We trusted the car would be safe there and went shopping.

The awareness download was abrupt and intense.

"Hey, who are you? How many are you? What are you doing here? You're not welcome in our car!" I then touched my body and I asked it to release everything it had tapped into from anyone during our trip to Brussels. As my body was unwinding, the sugar crave disappeared. The choking smell of the marijuana faded as well.

"Maybe next time we ask a question before throwing ourselves on food," I mumbled.

"I told you that you didn't need sugar. You didn't listen to me."

"That was not a question, my dear wise husband. That was not a question!" I continued teasing him with a smirk on my face, pushing his glasses higher up his nose. "So, now, let's ask a question… We've had demons, drugs, alcohol… what about sex?"

"How much?"

I burst out laughing with the lightness of someone who has just acknowledged that there is nothing in this world that can take our joy away - not even less conscious entities.

The Lady in the Channel

I've been living in Belgium for 17 years. And I have to confess that it took me some time to get along with 'the energies of the place'. I love Brussels, and yet it used to drain me to go into the city, and be among its people.

It was always so busy; so crowded; so intense.

I remember my first trip to Brussels city centre. My husband (back then, my lover) wanted to impress me, so he gave me a sightseeing tour of my "home" to be. We were driving along the channel when all of a sudden I panicked.

"What if he leaves me here? I wouldn't f*cking know how to get anywhere from here!" I thought to myself out loud. A sort of desperate uneasiness grabbed hold of me. My mind made a note: "You are not safe. This is a dangerous place."

He - playing the villain - heard me and laughed. Every time we would pass by that spot in the future, he would say, "Imagine if I had left you here!" and we would burst out laughing.

However, that nasty feeling of panic was present with every drive along the channel at that particular place.

Until... it wasn't.

A few months ago, on the same route, I had the same feeling and my husband was waiting for me to repeat the phrase, "Oh, my goodness, if you left me here...."

All of a sudden, I was out of breath. I got dizzy, and my vision blurred. I was gasping for air desperately trying to unzip my winter coat. I removed the safety belt. I opened the window for air. My lungs would not open. I wanted to throw up, but there was nothing that would come out. Tears started running down my cheeks.

In the middle of my panic episode I shouted with frustration: "What is this? What do I do with this? What is this? What do I do with this? Whatever it is, more ease, please!"

It took a question and a demand: the information download was sudden and intense. There was a lady, middle-aged, confused, crying, and struggling to breathe, choking, and fighting for her last breath of fresh air.

"Kids, daughters." The information was still coming.

I launched all the tools that came into my awareness to keep me present and allow the space for this entity to be present with me.

When she calmed down I told her that she didn't have to suffer any longer. She was no longer trapped in the car that fell in the water. She was free to go visit her daughters if she wished or to choose to find another body and be close to them.

That fraction of a second of sheer sharp clarity was priceless.

She left at peace. My breathing came back to normal. And I never had that feeling of awkwardness ever again.

My husband witnessed it in silence perceiving the energies unfolding. He perceived the intensity of the exchange as well. I didn't mind what he was thinking or what he would say about it.

I owned this awareness and the accuracy of my entity awareness.

It only took me 17 years...

Snuffy

It's been 24 hours since I left our dog Snuffy at the clinic. One week before she had some kind of a stroke which temporarily paralyzed her front right foot. She stopped on the way back from the park and threw up convulsively in the middle of the street. I didn't panic, but I knew that something was not quite right with her body. I called the emergency vet immediately. The doctor arrived within 15 minutes and began examining her thoroughly.

I sometimes refer to Snuffy as being my 'Shmooffy-pooffy", "Mufkin", "Yoga-dog", or "Moose-Poose". Sometimes she's just a spoiled brat who I happen to love beyond words. Like every dog lover, I am very fond of her and we have learned to live with her nasty habits of sleeping on the freshly washed clothes, or scavenging the trash bin for food scraps, going in and out of the house 50 times in 3 hours, or asking us to open the door to the garden and then close it after she's back. And then there's my nasty habits of trimming her nose fur, squeezing her, and blowing air into her ears. We tease each other and this makes us happy.

Seeing her losing her joyful way of being in a few hours time stirred a lot of uneasy feelings for me as well. I was not desperate. I was simply pragmatic.

I was watching the vet trying to establish what went wrong with Snuffy. The more the doctor got nervous, the more the dog became sick. She took a few blood samples to check a few basic values. They indicated the pancreas function was way over the limit. Snuffy had a fever as well. She received a perfusion with antibiotics and painkillers.

The next day we had an appointment with the regular vet. Snuffy got some medication. They continued the blood investigation as well, and then we were free to go home. By Monday, she looked like an inflated fur balloon, feeling uncomfortable lying on her side. Her usually happy curled tail was now dragging on the floor. Her coat was messy and her eyes were alarmingly red.

I booked another appointment the next day.

***

"Oh, it's you!" one of the vets at the clinic greeted us. "I didn't recognize you at first. You are Lady Gombots," he exclaimed. "Oh, I'm sorry about him passing."

"It's okay", I replied smiling at the memory of the most extraordinary tabby cat that has ever populated this Earth. "Gombots was quite a handful."

"I agree. An amazing strong cat." The conversation fell flat when he asked me to put Snuffy on the metal consultation table.

It was then that the doctors agreed to have her sedated in order to take some X-rays. They wanted to get a better understanding of what was going on. An ultrasound would follow. It was an easy procedure.

Snuffy had a different plan. She was not having it, and was reluctant to let herself be taken care of. I could see her fight against the drugs with all the strength she had in her.

When she finally gave in and the doctors could have

her lie still on the examination table, the X-Ray revealed a tumour, which could not be detected by the ultrasound exam. Her pancreas was also severely infected and enlarged, which contributed to a general state of tension in all her internal organs. After having deliberated for a few long and excruciating minutes, the doctors asked me into the room.

I was waiting outside fully aware of the nervousness Snuffy aroused in the doctors. They cared for her and were truly handling her in the kindest way possible.

One of the nurses knocked at the door of the operating room and announced the arrival of a cat for euthanasia. My heart pinched for the owners. It reminded me of the last time I came in with Gombots two years ago.

***

I had brought Gombots in to be put down. I stood next to him and caressed him until he died. I perceived him leave his body and stand next to it on the table. A few seconds later, the doctor declared him dead.

I used to be so scared of death, dead people, and dying creatures, yet Gombots invited me to acknowledge the beauty and the peace of passing away. I felt honoured that we chose each other to celebrate our lives together and his death. He had been a living example of leadership on four legs, challenging me to step up and be present with my fears and my doubts.

Gombot's health had been degenerating for more than a year. According to the doctors, he had less than 3 weeks to live. They discovered a tumour in his stomach and his heart was enlarged. He also was having a hard time breathing properly. The doctors suggested we allow him to die in his sleep. I asked to have a moment with him.

"Gombots, is it time?"

"No, not now." His answer was loud and clear. I took him back home despite the doctors' advice not to. He lived for more than a year until one morning, while sunbathing on the windowsill in my office, he pulled my energy in.

"Is now the time? You've always been a strong cat. Would you like to go look for another body?" His body relaxed. His breathing slowed down. I knew he could struggle for a few more days but to me his choice was clear. We took him to the vet, honouring our care for him, and his immense loyalty towards us.

When we reached home, both my husband and I perceived his presence on the sill. He looked disoriented and confused. I realized that the amount of drugs in his system prevented him from grasping the new reality.

"Hello, my friend." I asked for all the drugs from his universe to be dissipated and released. "You died. You don't have a body any longer. You are free of pain. It's okay. You can go. You can go look for another body if you wish." He vanished and never came back... until one December evening.

My son had a particularly rough day at school with his schoolmates bullying his best friend. He was upset and on the verge of breaking down in tears when I offered him an Access Bars® session.[6] He sighed with relief, sinking deeper and deeper into the massage table. He was melting with our new cat purring on his tummy when he said:

"Gombots was the best cat ever. He loved only me. Ary (our new cat) loves the others too. But Gombots was only mine."

"Do you miss Gombots?"

"Sometimes. And sometimes he comes to visit."

"Really?"

"Yes! He comes during the night. He steps over me and sits on my belly and looks at me."

"Does he talk to you?"

"Aham", he nods.

"With words?"

"Oh mom, this is not a movie", he adds rolling his eyes. "He doesn't speak! What an idea… He puts the words in my head telepathically."

I gulp.

"Why is he coming?" I was playing the cool parent, yet truth be told, I was melting with the acknowledgement that my kid had found the space and the courage to talk about his dead friend. "Are you calling him?"

"Sometimes. Sometimes he comes by himself. He misses me."

The conversation ended as abruptly as it started and he fell asleep.

I knew somehow Gombots was watching over Snuffy as well.

∗∗∗

"We know you're not going to like this, but Snuffy is in a lot of pain right now. She requires more than a normal dose of painkillers. Her body needs to relax, therefore we suggest she stay here with us, under observation for 24 hours. We will know more by tomorrow."

It was a no-brainer: what would create more? I knew that Snuffy's body had been stressed out because of the pain. It played on her mood as well. I didn't blink. I agreed. I kissed her while she was loudly snoring asleep and I promised her I would pick her up the next day.

Strangely enough, having Snuffy in the clinic opened up a space of ease for me as well. I fully trusted the doctors and her. I knew that she was perfectly able to choose for herself. I also knew she had amazing healing abilities which were not from this world.

When I returned the next day, she looked at me like I was a stranger… as if she didn't recognize me. My first thought was that she was punishing me for leaving her alone. There was also something in her eyes that I could not fully pinpoint. There was this expression of a puppy dog that would turn its head towards anything that moved and be distracted by the slightest sound.

We took a walk to our Magic Forest later that day. She was different. Maybe from the drugs? After all she had been receiving morphine just 24 hours previously.

She was walking next to me stopping every 5 steps confused, as if she was waiting for instructions on what path to take. This was odd, because we were walking our usual route.

I observed her closely. Her posture changed. She seemed surprised to discover that she could move and go about the beaten path. "What is this?" The moment this question reached my world, I knew.

"Snuff?" She stopped in her tracks and looked up into my eyes. "Hey, stranger, who are you? Who gave you this body? Will you please leave this body and go look for a puppy body?" She broke the eye contact and stayed put. We continued our walk.

When we reached home she emptied her water bowl and curled up next to me on the couch. I rested my hands on her body inviting her to connect to all the energies my body was gifting to her so that she had much more ease in her body.

She fell asleep. I knew she was back in her body. And, my body finally relaxes.

Helga

As much as I love travelling, I have to confess that I am quite a nervous flyer. I've always been. I remember the first rudimentary flights from Baia Mare, where I used to live in Romania, to Bucharest in Antonov aircrafts that made me throw up in my parent's lap every take-off and landing.

To be honest, I am not sure who was really sick and to what extent I was just materializing something that my parents were feeling. What I know is that every time we had the luxury to take a plane to go to the seaside, I would be horrendously ill for days afterwards.

Even so, one of my biggest dreams ever was to fly

long haul trips. The longest flight I have taken to date was from Brussels to Brisbane with a stop-over in Dubai. Truly, comfort and less crowded cabins make a huge difference in the flight experience, but so many times the shared experience with the economy passengers and the awareness that comes from being amongst them is priceless.

I was returning from a class in Costa Rica. Together, with a few of my fellow colleagues, we boarded the same flight to Europe. It was a cloudy evening and we were having a hard time saying good-bye to the nurturing experience of *pura vida* we had lived for a week.

The aircraft was parked right in front of the wide windows at the end of the San Juan Airport terminal. It has always fascinated me how a huge machine like that could lift from the ground and float over the clouds with so many people on board and only two pilots.

The captain was already on board. Check-in had just closed and we were now waiting patiently for the boarding call. I was standing alone, far from my chatty friends. I was not in the mood. All I requested was an empty seat next to me, and a good night's sleep. There was this crankiness in my world that simply didn't match anyone else's energy.

When they announced boarding, I joined the queue as far at the end as possible to limit the interaction with the people on board. I hated it when people would go past me, push their bags, stop in the middle of the aisle, and wait for their friends to see their signs that they had reached their seats, while everybody else had to stop at the same time. Then, there were the 'sorry' and 'excuse me' and 'no worries' that followed. I just wanted to sit down and take off.

The check-in agent checked my boarding pass and, as I was walking down the bridge, I felt this intense pull from the head of the plane. I turned my head and stared at the small windows just to see if anyone was watching me.

"Hi, what's your name?" I asked in my mind. "Are you a girl or a boy? Are you happy? Is this a good day to fly? Is there anything I can contribute to you? Have fun and land us safely! I know you're doing a good job!" I was talking to the airplane, which I perceived as having this mother-like energy, protective and caring. I smiled for the first time during the evening.

I finally reached my allocated seat in a high state of irritability, which increased dynamically when I realized that the plane was fully booked and there was not a single seat available for stretching my legs a bit. Moreover, I was sitting next to a guy who was taking his time to crunch on some nuts, which annoyed me beyond any of my tolerance limits.

I sat down, pulled a blanket over me, and cursed in my head the idea of taking this flight back home. I could have stayed one more day in Costa Rica. What was the rush?

Within 5 minutes, the guy stood up and made way for this young beautiful woman who looked scared and was on the verge of crying. I knew why I was on this flight beyond any cognitive logic. She sat next to me looking anxiously out of the window. When the plane started moving on the ground, she suddenly turned to me:

"I am scared!"

"Oh, boy," I thought, "Out of all the people on the plane, did she really have to come sit next to me? I'm not going to dive into her fears and clean shit up. No way! I'm sleeping."

"No worries, everything is going to be fine!" I replied turning my back to her and leaning my head against the window.

"Please!" she begged me with a frail voice. She

reached out for my arm in a desperate attempt to hold on to something stable.

I looked her in the eyes. There was so much fear in her world. I knew I could process it, but she was holding on to it as if it were real and true.

"Would you like me to hold your hand?"

"Yes, please. You don't mind, do you?"

"I can do this, but I would like to ask you something in return. Would you be willing to take a deep breath and imagine that you become bigger and bigger? It's like your body is still the same but your being is getting bigger and wider. You might want to go beyond this plane, around the earth, reach up in the skies."

The plane started to accelerate for take-off. She was clasping my hand so tight that her knuckles became white.

"Breathe in slowly and exhale slowly. You can do it. And now expand. I am here. I am holding your hand." She closed her eyes and held her breath. Panic was surging from somewhere I could not reach. "In and out…" I kept repeating until her body relaxed, her shoulders dropped. The plane left the ground smoothly, and she didn't seem to notice. When she reopened her eyes she smiled timidly and asked me to keep holding her hand for a while.

"Are you still afraid?" I asked.

"Yes," she mumbled with tears rolling down her cheeks. "I don't know," she replied.

"And if you knew, what would you then be afraid of?" She looked at me with a puzzled expression. "Did anything happen to you on a plane?" I continued.

She nodded. "But not to me… to my friend…" she was sobbing. "My friend died in a plane crash. Every time I step onto a plane I am so scared I will die like her. It must have been awful."

"Is your friend here with you?" I asked in a reassuring tone of voice.

"Yes!" She looked at me with big wide eyes trying to figure out where her answer came from.

"Would you like to talk to her? What was her name? Is there anything she would like to share with you?"

"Yes, yes…Helga… she was 16 when she died."

"What if you asked her if she knows that she died?

That she no longer has a body?"

"Can I do that?"

"Try it, see what happens. I'm sure you talk to her all the time. Why would this be any different?"

"How did you know?" she looked at me suspiciously.

"Well it happens to me sometimes too. I talk to my mom, and she died a few years back. You don't have to speak out loud. She knows you can perceive her and she hears your thoughts."

"She doesn't know she died! She thinks we are going to crash! Oh, God, are we going to crash?"

"No. She is just reliving the crash all over again. Could you tell her that all is fine now? She died. She left her body and that terror does not exist anymore."

"She's calmer now. What do I do? What do I say?"

"Nothing. Just be with her. Maybe tell her that you miss her and share how beautiful your life is with her having been in your life. Can you do that?"

Her hold on my hand loosened and I could perceive a smile on her face. I asked for the drama and trauma around the spirit of Helga to fade.

"Is there anything else Helga would like to ask from you? Is it her time to move on?"

"Yes!"

"Would you like to help her find her way to the other side and make a different choice?"

"Yes."

We cleared the entity of her friend together. There was a big sigh of relief that startled the flight attendant. She was serving beverages before dinner.

"What just happened?" the girl asked me in a low voice.

"Well, what do you know happened? Are you still afraid? What if that fear was not yours to begin with? What if it belonged to Helga?"

She fell quiet. She released her hand from my hand. Tears were rolling down her cheeks.

"Thank you. I don't know you. I don't know your name, but you were here for me. Thank you so much."

She fell asleep for the next 6 hours. When she woke up she almost screeched with surprise.

"6 hours! I can't believe this! I never sleep on airplanes! This is a miracle!"

I loved her enthusiasm, but I still wanted to sleep.

"You're welcome!" I turned on the other side, smiling at the beauty and greatness of entity awareness.

I Love Brazil

I love Brazil. I love its people! I love the food and the rhythm of life there. The colours, the smells, the steaks! I adore their caipiroshkas too!

I remember my first trip to Brazil was for a class in Sao Paolo. The connection flight I was supposed to take from Zurich to Sao Paolo had been cancelled right in front of my eyes while queuing for the second security check at the gate. There was a lot of commotion that evening in the airport, and a lot of frustration too. I managed to switch to an interesting point of view about the situation quite smoothly though.

I opened my phone and did a Facebook live saying

that I was among the fortunate to not have any emergency to attend to. I literally said that there might have been people dying and the loved ones could not meet them before the end. That saddened me. It enraged me more than anything else. In any case, the worst that could happen to me was to be late for my class.

I still get the goose bumps when I think about it...

The next day I was embarking for my destination together with a fully packed plane of unhappy people. I was fine. More than fine. Yet there was this uneasiness in my world which I could not place. It felt as if my eyes were swelling inside their sockets and this annoying pressure would not go away. But, hey, Swiss chocolate is always welcome on long haul flights and I had received a generous supply from the flight attendants. That should have been enough to make me happy for the next 14 hours.

Yet, the buzzing pressure inside my skull wouldn't cease.

"Who does this belong to?" I wondered. "Not me? Well, thank you very much. I am sending it back!"

I tried to keep me entertained with a movie on demand. I hated it. It made me so sad, and it was supposed to be a comedy. I took out a book. It bored me. I took out my notebook. There was nothing to write. I didn't listen to any of the audios I had prepared for the trip, because my ears were buzzing.

Utterly annoyed, at some point I stood up to stretch my limbs and revive my body. I stood in the galley for a while exchanging smiles with fellow travellers, looking outside from the emergency exit door window. We were gliding on the fluffy clouds and no one could tell there was anything underneath them. It was a smooth flight and I appreciated it deeply.

There was a group of people in the aisle chatting loudly and having fun. Small empty bottles of alcohol were accumulating in the trash bin while the decibels were getting higher.

Among those people was a lady who I was pulled towards like a magnet. She was silent and looked worried, or maybe sad. I could tell she had been crying.

"I'm glad we're on this plane," I started. "At least we don't have technical problems to worry about."

She nodded.

"I'm Selena." I said, offering her a chocolate.

She smiled timidly out of courtesy.

"Have a smooth flight." I wished her, about to return to my seat.

"Thank you," she answered. "I love Swiss chocolate."

I watched her open the silver foil wrapping, bite one tiny corner of it, and close her eyes, sighing and crying.

I didn't know what to do. She was not exactly willing to talk to me; yet, she was somehow asking me silently to stay. I moved closer to her in the galley pretending I needed a glass of water, giving her the space to make up her mind if she wanted me there or not. I didn't know what it was, but I couldn't leave!

"It doesn't matter anymore if I have a smooth flight or not… not now. I'm late anyways." She took another bite of the chocolate looking down as if her eyes were piercing the floor. I knew she was trying to control whatever bothered her. Maybe anger? Frustration?

"Late… for what?" I inquired cautiously.

"For saying good-bye."

A cold current thundered through my body making

me jerk with intensity.

My nose got cold, my throat dried, and my chest seemed congested. I took a sip of water while acknowledging what was going on in my body.

"He died last night after they announced the technical problems with the flight. I made so many efforts to see him before it was too late. I didn't want him to die and think I didn't love him. He must have felt so lonely!"

I was silent. My symptoms suddenly made sense. There was nothing wrong with my body. I was just picking up the distress of… the man standing at the end of the corridor. His presence became more obvious to me.

"My father and I lived together for a long time. I was the one to take care of him, but when we ran out of money I had to leave him with my sister. She lives in Sao Paolo and the doctors said that it would be better for him to be somewhere in a milder climate. I haven't seen him since, and I promised I would go and visit. I worked two jobs all this time to send my sister money to be able to take care of him."

She was sobbing consumed by guilt wiping her nose with her hands.

I smiled. "That's a very elegant way of doing it," I blurted out of nowhere pointing to her hands.

She looked me straight in the eyes, puzzled.

"My father used to tell me that all the time. How did you know?"

I didn't. The information just poured in.

She said, "One time I had been in a fight with a boy from across the street. I must have been 10 or something. When I came home, I sat on the back door porch and cried for hours. He had called me names and had made fun of my family. I had smacked his face and then felt so bad for him. I was raised to be honest, caring and kind, but he had crossed the line. Later that afternoon my father found me falling apart in the back yard. He didn't say much. He had just observed me wiping my nose with the back of my sleeve. He said, 'That's a very elegant way to wipe your nose clean!' He hugged me and I knew everything was fine. There was no sorrow in the world that he couldn't melt away with his hugs."

The heavy presence at the end of the alley seemed to lighten up.

"I'd say that he's melting away your sorrow right

now, wouldn't you?"

She lifted her head, looked me in the eyes, and sighed.

"In fact he is," she acknowledged enthused. "I have this feeling that everything is going to be fine!"

"What if he didn't leave without saying good-bye? Could it be that he is here with you until you are ready to say good-bye? If you knew that everything is possible, what would you love your father to know, wherever he is now, next to you or in a different world?"

"That I loved him so much!"

"Well, what if you closed your eyes for a second and listened. What would he be telling you?"

There was this soothing silence and space that opened up in the kitchen galley of the Boeing 747 flying from Zurich to Sao Paolo that no words can encompass.

When she opened her eyes, they had a sparkle of joy in them. She seemed to have been coming back from afar, now holding a different truth than the sorrow of having been stolen the right to say good-bye to the most beloved person in her life.

I moved back to my seat and we never spoke again. I don't know her name. I simply wish for her to know that everything is going to be fine if she chooses it to be.

***

After arriving in Sao Paulo, I made my way to my class happy to see and meet my Brazilian friends. It was a hot sunny afternoon and we decided to enjoy the lunch break of our class in a different setting than the hotel lounge.

They took me out to the busy popular side of Sao Paolo and invited me to have a taste of a somewhat less polished side of the Brazilian lifestyle.

When the taxi stopped in the middle of the road, I began smiling, perceiving my body capturing all these new flavours and energies and people and atmosphere, becoming more and more joyous with each step into the crowd.

On one side of the street there was a flea market, and to our right there was a line-up of restaurants and intriguing places to go have lunch. I could not make up my mind, yet I somehow felt reluctant to go to the flea market. I thought it had been something about my dress – too in your face perhaps – even though

Sao Paolo's popular streets are richly colourful. It was my expansive energy that met less friendly eyes... It didn't matter. I was there to enjoy.

We finally sat at an indoor terrace and ordered traditional food – those black beans, man! I flooded it all with some caipiroshka and beer, and then we continued our adventure in an artisans' warehouse. I felt like I was in heaven! I could watch the artists at work, and enjoy first-hand what they produced. Pure delight!

I remember one of the girls having a glimpse at my face while I was trying on a gorgeous pair of handmade earrings that somehow made my face change. It was true. I looked at myself in the mirror and saw a totally different person. There was this immense energy wave of joy and exaltation coming out of all my pores. I didn't have an explanation for it, but it felt so good.

All this time, I also had a sense of being watched. I would keep turning my head behind me as if someone were piercing my back with laser beams. Yet, I couldn't see anybody.

When the break was over, we returned to the class. I started to feel sick. In fact, I felt so sick that at some point I could no longer move. I had gifted the

Access Bars® to a fellow participant and immediately after that my back seized. I could not move; I could not breathe. I felt dizzy, and the only thing I could think of was that it must have been food poisoning. However, all of the girls at lunch had shared the same food and the same drinks and they were fine.

I must have been looking pretty desperate when a friend of mine approached me and asked me if there was anything she could contribute to me. I couldn't speak. My jaws were so tight that I was afraid I would not be able to open them any longer. On top of it all, there was this panic in my world, and deadly thoughts were hovering about my head. I knew they were not mine, yet none of the tools and questions that I used seemed to work. "What the hell was this?"

Things were getting a bit too significant, heavy, and out of control... and not in a good way.

I lied down on a massage table in the classroom hoping to allow my body to rest and release the overall tension. It hurt even to lie flat on my tummy and all I could do was moan with pain.

My friend touched me gently on my back and it felt like she had pierced me with a sword of fire. I thought I was losing my mind. I knew something was definitely off. We both continued to ask questions out loud: "What is this?" repeatedly until we both exclaimed at the same time, "Entities! Psychic attack!" My body jolted on the table as if someone had just did CPR on me.

From that moment on we both knew what we were dealing with. We took out our tools and started clearing all the demons and all points of view I had, from all past life connections with whatever I had been and done in Brazil that kept me out of my awareness, and in that loop of agonizing pain.

It took approximately 5 minutes for the pain to go away, for my mind to clear, and for the ease of awareness to land into my world. It felt like the whole world had revolved on its axis simply by shifting the energies I had stepped into. Man, these tools work!

Entities of the Earth

I've just boarded the flight back home from Buenos Aires. It's going to be a 16 hour flight to Zürich, and I already ask my body for ease with this part of the journey.

I acknowledge the apprehension in the air. I look around and I perceive peoples' worries and anxiety. It catches me off guard to be diving into their world once again.

"I know better than this," I mumble.

I am sitting comfortably in my seat. There's an empty seat next to me and I am smiling at the prospect of stretching my legs and having extra space for the food.

50 minutes after we take off, the plane starts to shake. The 'seatbelt on' sign blinks incessantly. The pilot asks all of the passengers to keep seated. We are facing powerful turbulence ahead.

We've been up in the air for a few hours, cruising through air holes and forceful currents. Crew and passengers start to become exhausted by the constant pumping of adrenaline in our bodies.

There's such a dense tension and fear in the air that you could slice it with a knife.

I am getting more scared by the minute, and I know this is not where I want to be. It will not create ease for any of us. Time seems to slow down. A minute turns into an excruciating hour.

I take a deep breath and ask myself to be present. "What can I contribute here? What do I know that would assist in this situation?"

I listen to the sounds of the plane. The engines are running full power. There's something like a subtle resistance. It's almost like it is forcing itself ahead while continually facing a membrane of resistance. It makes tremendous efforts to advance.

From the corner of my eye, I catch a glimpse of the wings. They seem heavy, burdened, and weak. They seem to carry an invisible weight that reduces their flexibility.

It happens regularly that entities who would like to travel congest themselves in airplanes or travel hubs, because they are stuck with the idea that it's the only means of transportation that they can take to reach any destination.

It doesn't take long for me to connect with them and remind them that they don't need an airplane to fly; they can just transport themselves in the blink of an eye.

The effect is subtle and immediate. The plane gains height, but it's still struggling.

I close my eyes and expand. I ask to have a clear view of what is going on. I'm riding on the plane's nose cheering it and encouraging it.

By this time, the passengers have become restless and fearful. Out of nowhere, summoned by all the dark thoughts of the people aboard, demons appear in waves. The plane is incessantly shaking and bumping.

I reach for my phone and play the demon clearing silently.

I observe that I am losing patience. I am expecting things to calm down, and I switch from tool to tool instead of being present.

"What is it? Universe show me!"

An image is downloaded into my world: it's like a picture of the plane taken from above pushing against a network of energetic cords while it is attached itself. It looks like a giant fly caught in an energetic cobweb.

And I know. This is not about the weather, winds, planes, or people... it is more than that.

I asked my barriers to go down and for my energy to expand past the 30 000 feet in the air that we are and all the way down to 30 000 feet into the Earth. I expand more than I have ever have before. I reach far beyond my mind.

From this space of ease and peace I connect to the entities of the Earth in Brazil, and I ask permission to leave the country and to carry with me the treasure of awareness they have granted me while on my visit, and to share it with the world. I am asking for their contribution to travel safely.

"I am humbled and grateful for my experiences here. I will be back. I know it. And right now I ask to be reunited with my family and beloved ones. Can you please contribute to a smooth flight for all of us?"

I must have fallen asleep while waiting for their response. The plane found its course, and before we know it, the stressful hours are forgotten. I wake up from the sound of the seatbelt sign being turned off. I look at the map in front of my eyes. We're flying over the Atlantic Ocean.

"Permission granted."

"Roger, that!" I smile knowingly.

Russia

I'm visiting St. Petersburg. There is a team of absolutely magnificent people taking care of me and ensuring I enjoy my stay. It's late November. Strangely enough, the weather is dry. There's no snow. I wish I could have visited the city in a snowy time. It must be beautiful.

I am rushing from the airport to the venue where I will be chatting to fabulous people in a meet and greet session. I am dreaming of the champagne I'll be drinking celebrating my arrival.

1 more minute and I would not have had the chance to talk to them.

Selena Ardelean

***

I'm sipping my coffee at the gate in Brussels keeping an eye on the boarding call. My drink is too hot and I am already thinking about the probability of having to throw it away because of the boarding. An announcement catches my attention: the flight to Prague is delayed by 20 minutes. My mind computes. This causes stress further down the line as my connection to St. Petersburg has only a 1-hour layover.

I scan the people sitting quietly and conforming. I can spot the ones boarding for my connection flight. They fidget; they search frantically on their phones; they assault the gate counter with a lot of questions without answers. The agent replies in the same tone of voice, "We will keep you updated as soon as we have information."

After 45 minutes go by, we are boarded and ready for take off.

Looking outside the window, my heart fills with gratitude for this magnificent earth covered in miracles that sustains our life. It's beautiful and soothing to know I am a being living on the Earth, even when I invent my struggles. It's such a gift to be able to be this joy and grace that the Earth invites us to be.

We're flying above the clouds. My mind wonders how many lifetimes I have lived in Russia. There's a strong sense of connection with and understanding of the land, of the people. And there's something more. It's a feeling of remorse and regret for having been disrespectful or oppressive towards the land and its people. Interesting.

I have never been to Russia before, yet Russian influences have been very strong in my childhood given I was brought up in communist Romania. There were historically tight connections between the two countries. To be honest, I felt safe with the strong, blunt, rough, and demanding appearance of what I would call 'a Russian'. I recognized those same traits in myself. I have always known that these were just labels from somewhere else together with the idea that Russian people should be feared.

"Maybe this trip we are finally going to get to know each other."

Just then, the flight attendant whispers something to the passenger in the seat right in front of me.

"But I'm flying to St. Petersburg. Can they wait for us?" I hear the attendant answering, "Yes."

It takes me a few moments to connect the information in my head. We are delayed. And I know we are not going to make it. Unfortunately there is absolutely no other connection available to St. Petersburg from Prague until the next day. I had checked all possibilities before choosing this one, willing to take the risk. This is one trip I am not going to cancel.

When the flight attendant approaches me, I ask him directly if there is any other connection available to St. Petersburg. He nods. He cannot tell. All of a sudden, all my plans cave in. 30 people waiting for me, the hosts, the hotel, and all the rest would have to be rescheduled. There's no way I can contact anyone of the team. I am literally 'in the air'. "Hmm, so now what? Who is available to assist?" I look up in the air asking for my entity friends to work their magic.

We land. The connection flight takes off right from under our nose despite our epic run through the terminals of the Prague airport. There are six of us. An agent guides us to the connection flights desk. I arrive first from the group. I am visibly irritated and the lady in front of me is obviously willing to go home, not to rebook us.

"What's your name?" she asks from behind the computer. I answer in a husky tone. She throws a new boarding card on the counter. "Gate 43, boarding in 20 minutes. Middle seat."

I take the boarding card, thank her, and rush to the gate. I look behind me. The counter is closed. The 5 other people are stuck waiting for a connection flight, and I am booked for my connection. I made it just in time.

"What a gift! Thank you!" I know this is a gift from my unseen assistants. I just have the most amazing team working with me.

***

It's been a fabulous encounter with kind and sweet people. We laughed; we cried; and we said good-bye laughing. I smile with the bubbly memory of the previous night.

I awaken to seeing white outside my window. "It's snowing!"

I jump out of my bed and grab my clothes. I rush to the bathroom, clean myself up, brush my teeth and… no, I cannot comb my hair. Joking entities must have had the time of their lives. My hair looks entangled as if I had combed it in 'rasta' style. I pull it up in a bun, have a look at my puffy eyes –

oh, well, busy night apparently – and I run down the stairs wearing only my dress and my phone. Snowflakes are tickling my face and my eyes and make me tear. Just before my make-up is completely ruined, I take a few selfies right in the middle of the street, confusing some angry drivers. It looks like I am the only one enjoying the snow. I laugh out loud causing people to stare at me. Wait! Did I just see someone smiling!?

It feels like the holidays to me, yet Christmas is still a month away. There's this expectation in my world and effervescent sense that I am about to receive a present. I have no idea what this is, but I totally love it.

I drink champagne for breakfast and enjoy the luxurious decor of the hotel restaurant. I can't help but smiling and noticing all the people passing by, greeting me, and willing to serve. I don't require anything actually. Still, it's a fun feeling to be served.

I'm going to have a guided tour of the Hermitage today. My host booked a private guide so that I am able to fully enjoy my visit. When I hop in the black Mercedes waiting for me in front of the hotel, I feel like a naughty girl princess spoiled with luxury, while the driver is cursing the bad traffic because of the snow. No, he doesn't speak English, but I am in love with his raw Russian accent.

Nothing prepared me for the magnificence of the place. From the wide open place in front of it guarded by an obelisk, to the grandeur of the palace itself, painted in vivid green with white and gold accents, all of it reminded everyone in its presence of the glorious Russian royalties who once used this building as their winter residence.

The museum is busy today. Hundreds and hundreds of visitors are waiting impatiently for their turn. I sneak in through a back door reserved for those accompanied by a private guide.

We are walking towards the main mirrored entrance when I stop breathing. All of a sudden, I feel annoyed with all the people walking around, nosing around, and being everywhere. I am asking for space. The guide is telling the story of Catherine the Empress who wanted to leave a long lasting impression with her guests. She asked for the stairs at the entrance to be high enough so that the female guests of her palace would not have to struggle with their elegant dresses while marching those stairs. She required that the experience be exquisite, creating a sense of space and of richness through mirrors and paintings.

"You know, these stairs are always busy. And you can book them for huge amounts of money one day a week in the morning to have your wedding pictures taken. Otherwise, it is almost impossible to find yourself alone here."

And there is this sparkle of silence. I hand the camera to my host and ask her to capture the moment. I am alone on the stairs. There is nobody walking next to me. I lift my dress and I climb the stairs slowly. A rush of energy flows through my spine up to the back of my head. I reach the top of the stairs and I know… I am home. It doesn't take long for a few tourists to barge into my awareness and burst my bubble. It is all I require to know where this fascination comes from.

When we enter the ballroom, I notice it is almost empty. "Very unusual," exclaims the guide. "Ask and you shall receive," I whisper, turning around in circles with my arms wide open. I am enjoying the precious space of golden, rich, luscious, wealthy energies I recall from other worlds.

The throne room silences me. It is imposing, demanding. My chin lifts up; my back elongates. All that is in that room demands presence and respect for the power.

I waltz through the rest of the rooms in awe. The guide jokes that I would have been a perfect Catherine, and I cannot stop myself from thinking… "I wonder…"

Later I sit at a table in a local restaurant devouring traditional dumplings. And I wonder again… Everything seems so familiar. And I am happy.

Paris

There's no place in the world that serves your croissant the way they do in Paris. It's soft, delicate, melts in your mouth, and when you savour it with a hot black coffee early in the morning, you no longer pray to get to heaven; you are in heaven.

Except for this morning though. My croissant tastes like cardboard, and my coffee resembles a concoction of dirty worn socks boiled in sewage water. I'm grumpy, cranky, and I am not willing to talk to anyone. I have decided that I am wrong; therefore, I demand to be left alone and simmer in my own self-judgment. It had been a tough start to the journey on the shores of The Seine. It's one of those mornings…

Stories of the Unseen

***

"Madame, are you sure you've got the right address?" the Uber driver asks me in a hesitant voice. "There is no way I can take you all the way through on a Friday evening." He apologizes scratching the top of his head. "You see how slow we advance. It's been half an hour for 2 kilometres. I'll get you a bit closer, but I can't take you all the way."

He drops me on the sidewalk, keeps the change, and leaves me wondering what direction to take. It's a late sunny afternoon. I am wearing my favourite long white dress with a palm leaves print showing generous cleavage. My white lace underwear is subtly visible under the fabric. Hanging onto my high heels, phone in hand and dragging my turquoise trolley, I seem to be part of the landscape. The GPS sends me to the right. I wander for a while on a sombre side alley until it opens on the street I am looking for. The sun falls on my back, and it lights the dark path between the centuries old buildings. It smells awfully like urine, infested walls, and mould.

As I walk down the street, I am painfully aware of the unwanted attention I am drawing towards me. My bag is too noisy; my dress is too revealing; my lipstick is too inviting.

Two women chat over the narrow street, leaning on the entrances of creepy looking doorways. One is fixing me with discoloured eyes while puffing from a hand-rolled cigarette. She swings her head in my direction to pull the attention of the other one. The corner of my eye records her spitting on the ground. The atmosphere is electric. I smile and make myself small and inoffensive.

"Qu'est-ce que vous cherchez… madame?" I hear a voice barking very close to my ear. I had not seen the third women approaching dangerously from my back. "On peut vous aider, peut-être?" She is asking what I'm looking for and if she can 'help' me maybe.

The tone of her voice makes my jaw contract. My defenses get activated in a fraction of a second. I am being hunted. "Oh, thank you! I am so grateful you're here. I am looking for the lock-key cupboard. It should be in the washing salon," I answer pretending I am stupid. The last thing I want right now is to get in trouble with them.

They all gather on my side of the walk leaning dangerously close to me. Their breath is unbearable: a combination of rotten teeth, garlic, cigarettes, and tons of alcohol. They sniff me as if I were their prey. I rush inside the washing salon, grab my key, and try to walk away. Unfortunately, I am walking in the wrong direction. They watch me disdainfully, scrutinizing every move.

When I turn the corner, I feel my butt relaxing and my shoulders drop. I am in tears. I still hear them shouting at each other, cussing and coughing the tobacco they've been puffing for years. It was like lifetimes of having been a cheap whore living on the street were barging into my reality from nowhere. It felt as if I would drown in judgment, shame, and disgust, all at the same time. I knew they wouldn't hesitate to harm me if they wanted to. I am upset and troubled by a sense of being wrong. Terribly wrong. How many lifetimes have I betrayed them by choosing something else? It doesn't make sense; but I know I have just shifted a probable nasty outcome.

My GPS reminds me that my location is on the right. I look around. My vision is blurry. I wipe my tears with my fingers cleaning the mascara dripping from my lashes. I am standing in front of a grid. A metal port is leading to a metal door. It smells like old trash cans forgotten to decay in the street. I get a bad feeling.

I open both doors and pull my bag up the spiralling stairs. I can hardly breathe. There's no draught of air. I keep climbing to the last floor. There are 3 doors next to each other. One is ajar. Spooky old children's toys fill in a huge hole in the door. Someone is coughing and spitting slime inside. My hands tremble when I open the door of the rented apartment. It's odd, unwelcoming, and unnerving. It doesn't look anything like in the pictures. The man next door argues with someone. They slam doors. My room reverberates. People are quarrelling in the street. Cars are honking. My heart races.

It's obvious I cannot stay here. And it's clear to me that this is a haunted building. My presence disturbs.

I call my husband and ask him to book me something else. It's summer in Paris in the beginning of August. Tourists are invading the city of romance. There's hardly any chance to find anything else. I'm crying. He tries to understand where I am and why I am so distressed. I just sob. He calls back in 10 minutes. He found a hotel.

I send a message to the owner of the apartment. He's not willing to reimburse me. He ignores all my messages. I tell him that he would have to come and pick the key by the hotel. He'll send a driver.

I had booked this place by myself. I didn't want to bother my husband with all kinds of trivial stuff. I am mature enough to book myself a decent place. Or not. I recall being pulled like into a black hole, when

I found the place. The pictures looked amazing, the price was good, and… something was off. Yet, I was drawn to it like bees to honey. The idea of my husband making fun of me is driving me crazy. All I can hear is "I told you so."

Fuck it!

I book an Uber. The driver looks at me suspiciously and when I step in the car he asks me if I am alright. "What is a lady like you doing in a place like this?" he wonders. My tears are unstoppable.

"Next time, madame, don't come near this place. You are lucky that I drove here, because no taxi driver is coming close to this place. Many tourists are fooled by the fact that you are close to the centre. You are, but not where you would want to be." He drops me at the hotel and makes sure I am at the right place.

Once in my room I rush into the small uncomfortable shower. I have to wash away the experience. The hot water sprinkles onto my body and allows it to relax.

"What was that all about?" I finally ask a question. It feels like I am hooked there, as if part of my being is still being haunted by the entities in the apartment and on the dark street. I cough violently, almost throwing up. My stomach is convulsing. My body is cramping.

I lie on my bed and cocoon myself in opalescent white light. It's soothing and relieving. I call in my team mates and ask them to watch over me while I sleep. I drift away in minutes.

I wake up at 5 am. Someone is having a discussion inside my room in front of the door. It's a man and a woman. "T'es con!" ("Asshole!") the woman laughs hysterically. The man pushes her against a wooden surface. I force myself to listen to the conversation. The voices come from afar. Then, they get closer and closer. I jump out of bed and turn on the night lamp. There's no one in my room. The voices disappear. It smells like cheap perfume and cigar smoke.

I check my door. It's double locked. I open the window and clear the air. My hair is a mess. My face looks tired. I drink a sip of water. I have 2 more hours to sleep.

When I finally walk out of my room in the morning, I am no way close to feeling good. I am exhausted. All I want is a coffee and a croissant. And space!

I sit at a café around the corner. The fresh morning air revives my senses. The waiter is pouring the second round of the infernal coffee while I stare lost in the memory of last night. He smiles. He points towards my sunglasses.

"Rough night?" he inquires amused.

"You wouldn't even begin to imagine," I reply.

"Try me. A cigarette?" he offers me his pack.

"I don't smoke," I reply serving myself.

"I don't either… I actually have no idea who I am smoking for."

It's my turn to smile: "Well, I know!"

We chat.

Greece

The heat is almost unbearable. The sun burns ruthlessly every square centimetre of unprotected skin. We have already covered ourselves in thick layers of sunblock and have made provisions for fresh water.

We leave the car to rest in a small patch of shade under an olive tree and we venture towards the archaeological park. We are at Asklepios: the home of the first hospital ran by Hippocrates. Cicadas deafen us. Their buzzing makes our internal organs hum in sync with their sound. They are loud and compelling. No conversation is possible without shouting at each other.

Just before the gate, cradled by the almost unbearable sound, two cats sleep lazily. They don't mind us. This is their domain. As far as they are concerned, we are the ones trespassing. The kids approach and pet them before I can say anything. I don't feel like saying anything.

We're one week into our holiday in Greece. It's the first time being here for all of us this lifetime. Yet, with all the comfort of the 5 star resorts we have booked, we have hardly enjoyed it. On one hand there are all these restrictions imposed by the authorities to prevent Covid from spreading. On the other hand, except for the absolutely breath-taking view of the sea in front of our window, there is nothing much to say about the resort.

My husband and I have had endless discussions about me being ungrateful, while I was arguing that there must be something else available to do on our holiday other than eat 3 times a day, drink plenty of wine at night…and that was pretty much it.

Within the first day of our stay, we had finished seeing all the attractions for kids. The offer was limited, and the resort a bit too crowded for my taste. Due to the fact that the hotel was at a safe distance from the centre of the Island of Kos, getting in and out of the premises was heavily restricted. The only ways out were either via a rented car or the local bus that made me dizzy just seeing it going up and down the needle turns on the mountain next to the resort.

It felt like we were somehow ostracized from civilization in this artificially sustained oasis of sunshine and sea view. I did adore the apartment and the terrace on the first floor of a separate hotel wing. It allowed a distance between us and the roaring partying crowd. We were also taking in the full blow of our downstairs neighbours who were drinking constantly and shouting at each other in the middle of the night. Even our sexy encounters were suddenly interrupted by one of them who would blast out on the terrace almost smashing the gliding glass door.

And they were not the only ones. Among the early birds on the chaise lounges by the pool, we could tell who slept outside, because they wanted to get rid of their hangovers with the only coffee being available at 7am by the pool restaurant.

I had enough of the food. I had enough of the wine. I had enough of the disturbing neighbours. I told my husband that we needed to get out of the resort before I lost my mind. It took a few days of nagging, zigging and zagging, until he agreed to rent a car.

Joy and freedom flooded the inside of our car the moment we left the hotel gates. It was as if we were escaping back into life. I had a look in the side mirror. My face had changed. I looked younger, resembling a movie character from the 60's, wearing a big straw hat and a thin fluffy top over my swimming suit. I put on sunglasses and a pouting face just for the fun of it.

We agreed to do the tour of the island. We stopped at magnificent beaches and enjoyed the surprises of the local beauty. It seemed that the sea was different wherever we set foot. We were all vibrating, sunny, and happy.

"Where should we go next?" I asked taking a brief look at the map. "What about Asklepios?"

"It's kind of hot now, but we can't go to the beach anyway. We would burn up on the towels." The visual of all 5 of us lying in the sun imprinted in the smoking towels made us burst out in laughter.

"Well, it's on the way to the main part of the island," I said checking the itinerary. "Maybe Asklepios, and then we can go eat somewhere by the sea."

***

We are standing among the relics older than 2000 years. The heat of the sun is reflecting on the dried earth enveloping us in a hot melting shield. The entrance of the park is guarded by an old, twisted, odd-looking pine tree. Dead barren pine needles crackle under our feet, releasing a subtle scent reminding me of the medicinal remedies my grandmother had on her kitchen counter. I ask the kids to behave and honour the place and the space. I'm kind of talking without really meaning what I am saying. I am absorbed by the energies of the place flowing through me from all directions.

The cicada bugs are fading in waves in the background. We climb the ancient terraces that are built in stone. The view of Kos Island is stunning. Cypress and olive trees ensconce this sanctuary of silence at the top of the temple. Knowing that I am walking across thousands of years of history in a temple dedicated to Asklepios, one of the Greek healer gods where Hippocrates himself used to see his patients and channel the right treatment in his night dreams, weighs this place with significance. I feel numbed by all the rules I have been taught on how to behave in such a place, and how you should show respect. All those regulations inhibit any sparkle of spontaneous manifestation of joy.

I ask my body to show me where it would like me

to sit. My steps bring me deeper on the top stoned plateau, in the shadow of some chatty olive trees, hushing and whispering with the breeze. A fallen column is in my reach. I caress it with my hands almost incredulous. I am touching 2 millennia of energetic vibrations imprinted in the column that has witnessed it all: the construction, the beginnings, the endings, the rituals, the ceremonies, the intrigues, the savant exchanges of medical knowledge, the prayers, the secrets, the gifts, the talents, the failures, the pain, the sorrow, the magic, and the miracles. They keep the mysteries engraved in them in the long deep carvings along their silhouettes. Will anyone ever know?

My feet vibrate; my voice is shaking. I lower my barriers and I pull energy from the ground. The buzzing intensifies. The cicadas are louder than ever. I ask my body to allow this pull with ease. I am looking at the ground and I have the distinct impression that the surface of the earth is undulating with the energies. I expand beyond anything my imagination has ever done before and ask to have access to the knowing and gifts and magic of all the lifetimes that have been lived in this sanctuary.

My body sighs and unwinds, relaxing and receiving. My head is empty; my molecules are fizzy. My perception increases. I'm pulled all of a sudden to my left. A cat is sitting at the other end of the pillar. Her gaze is intense. I lean forward towards her. She doesn't move. I get the message. She is the guardian of the place. I thank her for her job and join my family. The boys are having fun with some other stray cats. They haven't missed me. I look back. The dark grey cat is sitting still; it's golden eyes transfixed on me. I get it is time for us to go.

***

We're sitting at a table in the middle of a tourist alley veiled by acacias in bloom. It's a family restaurant where each member of the family has a role. They love their place and people love them. There's so much care and kindness in their food. I have been laughing ever since we sat down. My body giggles.

"This is funny," I laugh, coming from the bathroom. "I haven't farted all day!"

"Now, that's a topic for a meal conversation!" my husband bursts out loud too, sipping the fresh poured Retsina. The icy drops of water glide along the foot of the glass revealing the shimmer of the golden potion. It's a hot summer day with two hot people sitting at a hot table in hot Greece. Our eyes glimmer with gratitude for each other, for the place, for the space, and for the childish curiosity that revived the explorers in us.

I am intently aware of the organic orgasmic energy this land and its people are gifting us.

"Cheers," he lifts his glass. "Where to next?"

"Let's go to the natural thermes!"

When we finally returned to the resort, it was the middle of the night. We were all smiling. Again, with every step we took inside the domain, my body began to contract and bloat again.

"Body… it's not our job to extract peoples' insanity from their bodies. Let's have ease."

So, we did! Within 2 days we were venturing out again, daring to take a boat trip.

The Isle of the Bloody Ones

I've been waiting in front of the elevator for several minutes now. My patience is running thin.

We arrived in Corsica a few days ago, in an attempt at being efficient and mixing holidays with some of the classes I am keen to attend. The classes are not available online; therefore, I have decided to have a fun time with the kids and, at the same time, have an educational moment for me.

Oddly, I am edgy, irritated, and on the lookout for the right reason to pick a fight. All I care about is to be right and righteous. I cannot settle into the new apartment. I have had violent dreams for 2 nights in a row. I know that bad sleep doesn't make me the most enjoyable presence. I'm not making any effort either. Except for my coffee in the morning, everything is a reason to pick a fight. And, we are a family of five…lots of targets.

We're on the Îles des Sanguinaires – The Island of the Bloody ones. Our apartment is on the 6th floor of a residential building, with a small pool and a restaurant with pool terrace. At least the kids are happy, even though they quarrel about their diving goggles and forget their shoes before entering the building.

I am on my way back to the apartment from the pool ready to make a scene.

In the middle of the hallway, kneeled, with blood splashing everywhere, my husband is holding his head in his hands. The vision sends a shiver down my spine. My anger disappears. My brain is paralyzed by the view.

I grab him by the arm and we rush to the bathroom. I don't say a word. He's shaking. I clean the wound with fresh cold water from the tap. Blood is gushing out from the crack of his skull in terrifying amounts. He is dizzy and would like to sit down. Holding his head lowered down doesn't help. I urge him to bear with me for a few more minutes. I put a towel on his head and apply pressure to the opening in his head.

He sits on the end of the bed. His gaze is wary.

"What happened?" I asked.

"It's you. You're always rushing. I always have to catch up with you. I was walking down the hall and I didn't see the corner of the open window."

All I can say is, "I am not going to stop for anyone. Not even for you."

I walk out of the bedroom to clean the mess in the hallway. Half an hour later we drive to the pharmacy for some transparent band-aids and non-invasive wound care. We are silent yet blaming each other for what happened. I have a sense of something strange happening; yet, I don't have the words for it.

***

The class is about to start. The topic had intrigued me since my first encounter with the Talk To The Entities tools in a *Creation with the Entities* class. I can't remember anything from that class except that it was a trigger point for a major change in our life.

In May of 2018, I nagged my husband enough to take the car and drive to Paris for this awkward class for which I had no words. I didn't know why, but this class annoyed me and bugged me. It bugged my mind so much that I was in the state of mind where I was not stopping until I got what I wanted. Call me selfish; call me a brat. I just knew I had to be in this class. We all had to be in there.

We hardly talk on the way. It's early and the kids sleep through. The police spot us on the highway. Our car is pulled to the right. I have an automatic reaction to police and authorities that makes me lose my calm. This time I don't think. I ask of myself: "Lower your barriers... expand... pull!"

"Your driver's license and the car documents," ordered the policewoman with a harsh condescending tone.

I ask in my head: "Turn up the volume and pull through her…"

My husband hands her the documents. The kids are silent in the car.

"Do you know why we pulled you over?"

My husband nods. "Have I done something wrong?"

"You have obstructed a police mission. You didn't allow priority to the cars entering the highway."

"I'm sorry," my husband apologizes. "On any other highway, the cars that enter allow priority to the traffic…"

"This comes with a fine, normally," she said looking intently at the documents, trying to make up her mind on what steps to take next.

"Expand, pull, and make the incident infinite," I ask silently.

"I see you are not from Paris. I will let you go this time. Just inform yourself next time before you take La Périferique. Have a good day!"

***

A few hours later, the meeting room is packed. A large group of people are waiting for the facilitator to come in and start the class. I can't hear a thing. All I can grasp is entities… hmmm… bzzzz… Kids make a lot of noise at the back of the room. I fidget. I am not there even though I wanted to be in this class and did everything in my power for us to be there all together.

By the end of the class, I am disappointed. "I don't f*cking get it!" This had nothing to do with what I was expecting. I liked the energy of it though. Yeah, it had been a nice change of scenery.

We say good-bye and decide to take a walk through Paris. It's cold, but Montmartre always has breathtaking scenery to take in. There's this energy of a Bohemian lifestyle, local artists, live music, vivid terraces, and delicious food.

When the phone rings I pierce my husband with my eyes. He answers. I read the concern in his world. He scratches the top of his head, looks down, and tries to figure out the best solution for what he is asked or told. I can't hear the conversation, but I know it's about his mother.

"Yes, I am going to contact the bank on Monday," he ends. "Thank you. No, I have no clue what happened. Yes, yes, I will call you as soon as I know more."

When he turns towards me he looks sad and 10 years older, as if he had shrunk when he heard the news.

"What is it?" I inquire sensing the tsunami of judgment invading his world.

"Nothing…"

I stare at him. "What is it?" I repeat my question.

"Well, it appears that there is no money left in my mom's bank account. Her friend accompanied her to a cash machine and apparently there is nothing in the reserves found either. I'll have to check on Monday."

We both know that this is the last drop that would push him to finally face his mom's situation. She had always been a very strong and independent woman, who, from a physical standpoint, was in great shape, but she was losing her mind. We've had endless discussions about admitting her into a senior home with proper care and nurturance.

There have been several episodes including when she got lost on the street; she lost her documents; she forgot to eat and had her insulin shot which plunged her into a diabetic coma while locked up in her house; she had bruised herself – yet I knew something else happened there – and she didn't remember how it happened. She could not remember a conversation longer than 5 minutes. She would keep asking the same questions. Unfortunately, from a legal point of view, we could do nothing unless she agreed to move to the senior home.

We've been living a silent, yet present worry for a few years now, until her bank account had been robbed and no one had any explanation for it. Both my husband and I had a strong suspicion that she had been abused by an outsider, and that demanded that we be present with whatever we had been avoiding considering.

By Monday evening we know more, but the situation is not solved. Her state of mind will deteriorate, and we have to consider admitting her as a kindness to all of us. What if kindness is doing what works for everybody and not what this world tells you kindness is? She always threw tantrums when it came to the idea of living in an 'asylum' as she dramatically called the establishment, accusing us of being responsible for her death if we ever locked her up. And every time we would have a conversation, she would try to be a victim, or be this nasty, feisty, ready-to-punch person, or a small helpless girl, or the 100% professional presence, pragmatic, and devoid of any feeling.

We had discussed with her the possibility of one day moving her residence to a serviced apartment. Whenever she would agree to it briefly, she would change her mind with a ranting scene the next day. It seemed a hard road to take to convince her into something. There had to be something else that would work.

On her birthday, in June, we invited her to lunch, as we always have since I moved to Belgium. It's coffee time and my husband doesn't seem to have ease with bringing up the subject of the senior home. I wait silently for him to open the conversation. Coffee is the best excuse. She loves coffee; yet, she forgets how many she has had in a day.

"Would you like a coffee?" I ask pushing the button of the percolator.

"Yes!" She answers with enthusiasm. "No sugar. No, no, no. It's not good for your health. And my diabetes… no, no, no…" She gazes at the table caressing incessantly the lace underneath her saucer. She finishes the coffee in two gulps.

"Can I have a coffee, please?" she points with her head towards the coffee machine, completely ignoring the empty cup in front of her.

"Mom, you just had one."

"Oh!" she seems to notice the cup. "Well maybe a small one then," she continues in the well-known voice of an innocent helpless child.

In a matter of minutes, all her personalities show up driving the plot. It's as if the conversation is being run by a committee of disagreeing characters. She keeps asking the same questions again and again. I lose my patience.

I sit in front of her and I ask out loud, "Anne, can I please talk with the one in charge here?"

Her face changes, her posture shifts, and her back straightens up. She seems taller than the 145 centimetres she normally is. Her look is clear and present.

"Thank you," I say acknowledging that my ask was answered.

"Can you please help us here? It's no longer safe for her to live by herself. Would you please make the choice to go to the senior home? They are waiting for us in one hour."

"If you think that's the best thing to be done, then sure." Anne replied in an assertive tone.

A moment of presence, of no judgment, of receiving, and one precious tool'... Glimpses of the class we took in Paris barge into my awareness.

The Professional, as we called her, stays until my mother-in-law signs the documents allowing her residence to change and to clear the transfer of address. The director of the institution offers her a coffee and a chocolate allowing her to take in her decision.

"No, thank you. I've already had two. And you shouldn't offer chocolate to diabetes patients. I don't care that it's 70% pure cacao. It has sugar in it." My mother-in-law stands up and when the nurse walks in to show us her room she snaps. "What? Do you want me to punch you? I am old, but this doesn't mean I cannot smack your face… oh…but how can you do such a thing to an old poor woman? I am helpless and you are taking advantage of me. You don't have a heart."

It brings tears to my eyes. Still, I know it is the choice that creates the most, if not in this moment, then in the future.

***

It's a hot evening. Though I am barely wearing any clothes, I sweat abundantly. Wet patches appear under my breasts staining my fluffy dress. The same thing happens along my spine. I am embarrassed. My stomach feels heavy like a concrete block. The whole situation gives me cramps. Still I know…

I rush out of the meeting room. I still have 10 minutes before the *Introduction to Talk to the Entities* class starts. The impulse to vomit makes my eyes bulge out. Both toilets in the hallway of the building are taken. I rush to the elevator and make my way to our rented apartment. I cannot say a thing. I just desperately head for the toilet. I throw up violently, convulsively. My whole body is shaking. For a fraction of a second I rewind all the small incidents that happened up to that moment: the quarrels, the cracked head, the endless disagreements, the restlessness, the nightmares, me vomiting.

"Maybe you should cancel?" an annoying voice insinuates itself in my ears. "Maybe it's not a good idea? What if you have stomach flu? Would you like to be the one who spreads it to others?"

I recognize the voice. "I am not fucking listening to you!"

I wipe my face with a wet cloth and storm out of the house. I am 7 minutes late.

I find a seat in the second row. It's like a surrealistic movie. Almost all the participants are aware of entities. I have expectations and I know that this class is what I require to create change to fuel my life.

More than half of the class passes by me. I don't seem to be able to concentrate or focus. It's like my brains are melting, but there is this pregnant energy with something I am looking for. I do not have a clue what that is! My frustration grows more intense. It feels like a build-up nearing an explosion. I'd like to control it, yet I can't…

"A walk-in? Could this be possible?" All reality as I know it explodes in billions and billions of particles of lies. It's like finally there is light shining in the dark corners of my life. Someone knows what I have intuitively known for years! This is the information I have been looking for. Pieces of the puzzle fall into the big picture. The pixelated erroneous conclusions that led me to frustration rearrange themselves in a fraction of a second!

"I knew it!" I shout out ecstatic when we break for lunch.

The walk to my apartment seems to be the longest road I have ever had to walk. I hear the kids running barefoot on the slippery floor. They are soaking wet, rushing to grab lunch upstairs. Their laughter catches me off guard.

We take the elevator ride together.

"You look funny," says one of the boys, pointing at his brother who had deep marks of the goggles on his cheeks. Sacha turns around to look at himself in the elevator mirror.

"I can't see. I don't have my glasses," he jokes making a gruesome face.

The words roll out of my mouth:

"Sacha..."

"Yes." He answers calmly.

"How many are you?"

"Two."

"Who needs the glasses?"

"Him."

"Does he bother you?"

"Yes, sometimes. But I don't mind. He's just scared."

"Would you like to let him go, and have him find some other parents?"

"No." His answer was sharp and final.

"Why not?" I insist.

"Because he's my friend. Can you please leave me alone? I'm hungry."

Finally! After 6 years of torturing myself, there is a sense of release and relief in my world.

I have been judging myself for not loving my child, for not caring, and for being a psychopathic mom.

Sacha used to be my biggest love. He's the second of my three kids and until he turned 2 years old we had a sort of an inexplicable bond. He was a sweet, chubby, happy, and jolly little fellow. His only reason for making himself heard was to let us know he was hungry. He had the precision of a Swiss clock in his cute, round tummy.

When he turned 2 years old, he changed, from one day to another, without any warning. It was as if someone had switched my child overnight. I didn't have words for it. Just this deep knowing that my child was not mine. He looked the same. He had the same shape and size, but… he wasn't 'my child'. He started waking up in the night and banging at the door of his room. He kept having nightmares that exhausted me with sleepless nights.

I knew something was wrong, but I couldn't articulate it.

The day he stopped in front of the door and took off his clothes, minutes before school started, because he didn't have the right underwear on, I knew. I was not crazy. But there wasn't anything available to me to explain that horrible and incomprehensible change in my child. He was only 2.5 years old.

Our relationship has always been somewhat tense. I tried to make him what I once knew, yet he was nothing of what I would have liked him to be. No parenting skill I had at that time was working with him. I made myself so wrong. Soon, I was rejecting him because he was proof of what a failure of a mom I was. At that time, I wasn't asking any questions. I just had this heavy guilt and shame that I didn't know how to raise my child. To top it all off, my husband appeared to have a deep bond with Sacha, which also drove me nuts.

The sense of something else never left me. I trusted one day I'd have an answer. I just kept looking. And on a sunny August afternoon, on the Isle of the Bloody Ones, the truth exploded into my life. It shifted my perception from guilt and shame to the infinite yet precise awareness I had been having for such a long time, hovering in my world.

Nobody had changed my child. He made a choice to invite a different being into his sweet, jolly, happy body. It's not because he had a toddler's body that he could not choose to leave it. He just invited another one to enjoy life on earth as a highly intelligent boy with beyond this reality capacities and gifts.

How did I get so lucky to be his mom?

All Roads Lead to Rome

All roads lead to Rome, they say. Mine as well.

It's 7am and when I open my eyes, it takes a moment for the reality to settle in.

Last night I went to sleep early feeling tired and drained after the flight and the stress of finding my hotel. My husband had reassured me that it would be within walking distance. It was indeed. Yet, dragging my luggage on a paved street for a few kilometres in high heels made my brains buzz.

I must have been wearing inappropriate clothes as

well, as I was having a hard time breathing. I was taking short breaks to check the instructions on my phone and to catch my breath in an elegant fashion. I arrived at the villa neighbouring the Borghese Park, sweaty and unhappy.

The first thing that came to my mind about Rome was that I didn't like the city. It made me feel oppressed and small and ashamed and defenseless. It made no logical sense given that it was the first time I was visiting it.

My hotel room was luxurious. There was the silver wallpaper with a luscious baroque pattern, the black velvet cushions on a high bed, the big tall windows, a comfortable armchair to one side, a minimalist working space next to the window, and heavy draped curtains kept together by a silky interwoven belt. The view was wonderfully curated to the smallest detail.

I immediately started inspecting all its corners. A black marble with white veins bathroom and walk-in shower, thick soft and welcoming towels, toiletries, and a bathrobe. I felt like a princess. I searched for the coffee machine. It was a vital and indispensable element of decoration that would ensure a great start to the morning.

All looked beautiful, yet it felt… awkwardly off.

I took a shower and hid under my covers. I was hungry and anxious, and I could not bring myself to get my nose outside the room to look for food. I didn't want to talk to anyone, not even to my husband. It was all so weird, awkward, and strange. I googled some delivery sushi, and waited patiently for the nagging feeling of being unsafe to go away.

I sighed with relief when the concierge rang the bell bringing in my delivery sushi, and I surprised myself wishing to not have to leave the room ever. Strange.

I had a busy night. Of all nights I can remember from my travels, my first night in Rome was filled with bloody visions and awareness. I had been in battles; I killed people. I was killed, and resurrected; I healed miraculously; I led armies and died poor on the streets as a beggar. It didn't make any sense, and yet it did.

***

It's 7:30 and I am ready to roll. I sip my coffee watching the people walk by from my window. I am making plans for the day and do my best to delay the adventure until the city of Rome wakes up for tourists.

"I'll have breakfast first," I tell myself walking down the golden toned hallway to the kitchen. A young man is waiting for me and ready to prepare my eggs. We don't talk much. He's not allowed to entertain the guests. Fine by me, as I am not a morning person.

At 9 am, I am ready for adventure, curious to discover whether the feelings from last night are the fruit of my imagination or if there is any truth to them. The air is frisky. I can see my warm breath. My plan is to walk to the hop-on-hop-off station and have a tour of the major historical sights.

It's so early that I am the first one on the tourist bus. I choose a place on the deck and sit quietly listening to the audio guide. The bus stops here and there, picking other people up. I am fascinated by the buildings, by the stories, and by the bloody, salty, iron-like taste in my mouth. My body contracts, and a sense of defeat invades my world.

I can't hear the voice in my headphones, just a piece of information that gives me an indication of what I am aware of: Here, they used to bury alive the women who had sinned while the men were whipped to death. I have no idea where I am geographically. It seems that I took a dive into hundreds of lifetimes ago where I witnessed the torture of my lover. I was one of the sinners. My fate was sealed.

I snap out of it. "Girl, you've got a vivid imagination!" I try to soothe the sudden adrenaline rush in my body. It took me a while to relax. And when the bus stopped close to Vatican City, I suddenly decide to step out and walk on my own.

As I cross the Ponte Sant'Angelo – the bridge separating and reuniting Rome to the Vatican, it's like taking a walk of truth. Ten statues of Angels are watching your steps, scrutinizing your past, your present, and your future. I feel like I am required to ask permission to cross the bridge. I bow my head, then my body changes posture. I walk steady, tall, holding onto my purse with my right arm across my abdomen. It's not something I would normally do, yet my body seems to strangely relax while I continue to walk. I lift my eyes up to the painting-like blue sky. The Angel with the Whips is standing high in front of me.

My body knows the way. I don't have to ask for directions. I am carried towards Piazza San Marco. I walk in the middle of the way facing St. Peter's Basilica. The place is already flooded with tourists. My eyes register their presence, but I am not there with them. My journey pushes me forward.

I hear someone addressing me in an unknown familiar language:

"ты красивый. ты говоришь на русском?"

"Sorry. I don't speak Russian. Thank you!"

My long colourful jacket and rebel blonde hair do not go unnoticed. I instinctively run my fingers through my hair and smile at the struggle I had been through trying to comb it without success. The messy style looks appealing. People approach me. They talk to me in Italian, in Spanish, in Portuguese, in Polish, and in Russian.

"Who am I? When am I?"

I follow the signs to the Vatican Museum. My husband sends me a message. "You need to be formally dressed." Funnily enough, I chose a short dress for the day. "How am I going to pull this off with the guards who ask you to take your coat off?... What if I made myself invisible?"

I am granted permission to enter. There is only one thing I am here to see: the Sistine Chapel - a place steeped in the history of the Catholic Church, where popes have been consecrated…and, of course, home to Michelangelo's mind numbing work.

"Body is a symbol of hope," the audio guide resonates in my whole body. "I know this." My breath seems to spiral in an odd way. A soft voice asks us all to lift in prayer all those who are in need and the pope.

I have a sense of secrets coming out from behind closed doors. Undefined, unknown, undignified. I know something that I am not supposed to know. "What is it?"

I shorten my visit in a sudden burst of enthusiasm to visit the Basilica. I queue for ages in front of the security control. They make people take off their jackets. My dress is short, way too short. I blush. I perceive the energies changing. I am ready to have the guards lust after me if this is what it takes to get inside. It feels so natural. How many times have I done it before? How many lifetimes have I sneaked into Vatican City?

When it's my turn to pass through screening, the agent is distracted by someone far back in the queue. He doesn't notice me. I slide though the rotating metal system with ease.

I am standing in front of the Basilica filling my being with the energies of greatness of such an architectural presence. There's so much more to it than what meets the eye. The front entrance is open for tourists. I follow the signs guiding the path, and then I unexpectedly switch to my right. In a few moments, I am observing the changing of the guard in a lateral discrete hallway. I keep walking while asking myself where I am going when I notice an arrow pointing towards the Basilica panoramic view.

A few moments later, Rome lies at my feet – sunny, gorgeous, and immense. "I've seen this before!" I say out loud. A Japanese couple looks at me curiously. I realize I've been talking to myself. I wander on the roof of the Basilica for a while before I choose to go inside.

The discreet flanking door I'm going through opens on a narrow circular balcony running around the dome. The sun pierces the dark interior of the Basilica sparkling it with myriads of coloured prisms from the stained glass windows. The view seems so familiar. I tilt my head as if to check the inclination of some imaginary lines in my mind.

I peer down to the gorgeous mosaic on the pavement. I somehow see myself standing on the ground floor looking up towards the centre of the dome. I am dressed in white. I am a very religious man devoted to God and His service. I'm holding my hands in prayer. There's peace and surrender in my world. It smells like myrrh, frankincense, burnt candles, and something else.

I feel a push against the protective rail. Some kids are running and laughing. Their parents apologize for their behaviour in a clumsy Italian. I just smile back. I am back in this reality and choose to walk down the steep circular stairs as if stepping out of many pasts and futures at the same time.

I know I did what I came to do in Rome. Strangely, most of my visits in the world have not been about the reason I gave them, but about me reconnecting to places and instances that enriched my lives for lifetimes on end.

I sit at a café sinking in my chair. The sun plays on my cheeks.

"Ciao, che posso fare per lei, signorina?" A tall handsome guy is smiling down at me. Italian. He asks me if there is anything he can get for me. There's so much sensuality in the sound of this language.

"Un caffè corretto con panna." My response surprises him. "Certo! Un attimo!" he replies.

I sigh happy to know a perfect cup of coffee with cream is coming my way.

"Thank you, Rome! It's been a while! *Auguri!*"

A few minutes later I cross the bridge back to the bus station. I don't look back. My mission is fulfilled.

Turkey

A delightful experience, an explosion of taste and spices, belly dancing, and smoking!

If I were to read the ad panels at the airport I would get a very limited perspective on Turkish hospitality and the sweetness of the people. As tourists in Turkey, my husband and I have always chosen places that nurtured our bodies and tickled our senses. There has always been abundance, joy of living, and a lot of people who smoke.

***

I don't smoke. I taught myself how to properly smoke when I was 22 with a friend of mine. We were in a students' camp at The Black Sea. I was depressed with my dying first marriage, and out of revenge, I wanted to learn to smoke because he had taken up the nasty habit to accompany his new lover while still married to me.

We bought a pack of menthol cigarettes and sat on the beach, hardly knowing how to light the lighter. It was more applied theory than in any other class I had attended where you get a certificate at the end.

After having wasted the entire pack, we bought another one. This time a bottle of wine was of good help. And that was it. I only smoked occasionally, when someone was offering me one. I would never finance my own pack of cigarettes. I literally saw it as turning your money into ashes. Not fun.

I did however love to watch my mom smoke. She would puff, make the smoke travel through her lungs, exhale slowly through her mouth, and inhale it one more time through her nose. She looked like a dragon, which she was after all, but somehow that was one of the rare instances when I knew she was enjoying herself.

When she died, I bought a pack of cigarettes, and from time to time I would light one up thinking of her. She died almost 8 years ago, and I still have the pack.

My father used to be a heavy smoker as well. By 45 he was smoking two packs of cigarettes a day and drinking all sorts of alcohol, until he had a heart attack. He stopped smoking right that moment, cold turkey. From that moment on, no one was allowed to smoke in our house, not even my parents' best friends who visited once a year. He would always invite them onto the balcony or throw their packs in the trash bin. He wouldn't accept any excuse. Years later, by the time my brothers took up smoking, he was tired of playing the smoke detector.

"If you're stupid, it's your choice." And that was the end of any argument concerning smoking in the house. When he died, however, my mom took up smoking again. Sweet revenge or… something else? I'll never know her answer. I know mine though.

***

"Honey, on the way out, can we stop at the duty free to buy some cigarettes?"

My husband looks at me as if he had seen a ghost. I cannot blame him. After all, what was I aware of with my urge to smoke? Whose was it anyway?

He didn't mind me and continued walking to the exit of the airport. My palms started to sweat, and my heart started to race. I had this tremor inside as if I was having a glycaemic episode. "Can we stop to buy some sweets? I'm kind of shaking. And buy something to drink for the kids." My head was relentlessly looking for reasons to buy those damn friggin' cigarettes.

"I know you. You're like Pavlov's dog. You smell something and you have to have it! What has gotten into you with those cigarettes?"

"I don't know. I have to have them."

He finally bought me a pack of cigarettes, which I was planning to have last for the holidays, convinced that it was only a temporary crazy holiday idea.

We then moved forward to the buses that were taking the tourists to the hotels. We were among the "lucky ones" to get down at the end of the coastal tour. When we reached the hotel, the rooms were not yet ready. The kids were impossible, so I opened their bags at the reception. I gave them their swimming shorts and let them do the orientation tour of the resort by themselves.

After 30 minutes of waiting in the main hall for the

keys, I finally stepped outside in the merciless midday sun. My eyes were blinded by the light reflecting off the white pavement and the deep blue of the pool. I was looking for a seat in the shade when my eyes observed a cosy corner with comfortable couches facing the pool, yet secluded by a plant woven high fence. I made my husband a sign and sat down to chill under the electric ceiling fan turning full speed even in the open. It seemed odd, but hey, every place has its habits.

I have already spotted the ashtray on the table. "I'm invited," I grinned wickedly.

I lit a cigarette. The first puff tasted strangely divine. By the second, I was done with smoking, but I couldn't let it go. I continued to inhale slowly, hold my breath, and release the smoke while moaning with pleasure. That was weird. My husband was watching me from the distance intrigued by my unusual interest in smoking. One hour later he was joining me on the small patio, raising an intrigued eyebrow to the amount of cigarette butts dead in the ashtray.

"Can I have one?" he asked reaching for the pack.

"No." And I was serious. "You are a decent family father. You are a conscious righteous monk. Monks don't smoke. Only wicked hot bitches like me do!" I rolled my eyes blowing smoke into his face.

He snatched the cigarettes grinning. "I'm a monk… a perverted monk blowing one in the company of a hot bitch then." We laughed.

We noticed that every night after dinner we were drawn to that particular place in the evening where the couches were always taken and you couldn't see who was there because of the shishas or the regular smoke.

We soon ran out of cigarettes. It was no longer an issue to go buy some others. On the way to one of the little shops across the hotel, rushing to not miss dinnertime, I quickly looked in the direction of the patio. Nobody was sitting there, yet a cloud of smoke was hanging in the air in a strange way. When I looked again two seconds later, there was nothing left to be seen.

"Wait a minute… who am I smoking for?"

"Have you ever heard of smoking like a Turk?" No, it wasn't the voice of my awareness. It was my husband who heard me ask the question out loud. We burst out laughing.

"Cute, right?"

We quit smoking on the spot. The moment we acknowledged the entities inviting us to smoke, they stopped having any influence on us. The urge, the need, and the sweat have never revisited us since.

Anubis

I adore holidays for a lot of reasons and mostly because holidays are some of the rare occasions when I can just lie down and do nothing. Food is taken care of, someone else washes the dishes, and there's sun, sex, and lots of alcohol. From time to time you can squeeze in a massage or a spa treatment. You can read a good book by the pool, or you can get bored with having all that ease of abundance just for you.

Holidays have a direct effect on all my defense systems and shields I have forged with time to keep me out of my own body when shit gets intense, and I don't want to deal with it. I'll be honest. There were moments in my life when I would have preferred to be an ostrich: put my head in the sand and pretend no one was seeing my fluffy, out-of-proportion butt.

Holiday relaxation tends to flood my world with awareness, not all of it pleasant. But who says that being aware is something pleasant? That's the magic of it. Be present with what you are aware of and ask a question or two, depending on your mood and how much you're determined to suffer.

Turkey. All-inclusive resort. The beach is at my feet; the sun is on my nose. Holding my upgraded coffee in hand (yes, it has a generous amount of chocolate liqueur added), I am lazily lying on my chaise lounge waiting for the morning to pass and then go to lunch. There is nothing much to do in the resort other than just lie down motionless or splash in the waters. I am actually bored out of my mind and it kind of annoys me to be constantly in the presence of my kids. They are still a bit too young to be left by themselves.

A nice trim guy approaches me carrying a folder with promotional massage offers. His English is rudimentary, but his energy pulls me in. I say yes. Anything was better than what I was just doing – meaning nothing. I sign up for a week of cellulitis treatments and relaxing massages. I book my husband some sessions as well. We tried once to have a session together, in a different resort, and it was a disaster. I could not settle down, and he was snoring like crazy.

"Separately," I insisted.

We would take turns with the kids and we would let them know where to find us in case of an emergency. We knew that their only emergency would be to grab ice cream from the pool bar, and that was okay. I was actually waiting for them to have stomach aches, but that never happened.

I arrived early for my first massage session as they told me that there would be a tour, some additional information, blah blah blah. They were kind and helpful, but I just wanted the massage. When my masseuse arrived, all I could see about her was forced quietness, big hands, deep circles around her eyes, and a submissive smile. She did not speak English – well she did a bit – and I didn't speak Turkish at all. Later I discovered we could understand each other enough for a greeting and to indicate to me 'face up', 'face down', 'turn', 'harder?' and 'good?'

She covered me in a sort of very cold gel that made my body shrink with shivers. Then I was wrapped up in a hot electrical kind of blanket and was left "to cook" for about 1 hour. The temperature was rising gradually. I imagined that this is what a frog must feel like when put in a pot to boil at slow fire. It doesn't realize when it is cooked…and dead!

After about 30 minutes, I couldn't breathe properly. As my hands were wrapped in the blanket, kind of like a mummy, with only my head out in the air, I started to panic. I couldn't move. It flashed over me in a fraction of a second and flushed me in a wave of sweat. We stopped the session after 45 minutes and continued with the cellulitis massage while my body was still heated.

It was awful! I was restless and judging myself for… I don't even know what for.

That nasty sensation of panic kept following me for the rest of the day. I was literally considering cancelling my series of treatments, but I felt bad for the lady who had been so kind to me. "I'll give it another try tomorrow," I promised myself while committing to use some of the tools I had at hand to clear the space.

The next day, the unease was present from the moment I entered the treatment room. The lights were on. My masseuse was smiling kindly. My head was going "Oh, no!" The scenario repeated itself except that this time I didn't get into the 'oven.' I was just receiving a massage. Dark thoughts harassed me from all sides although my body seemed to enjoy her touch, which was surprisingly hard for a small woman like she was.

When I couldn't keep in place any longer, I started making conversation with her. She was a single mom working never ending hours to raise her child. Summer was the only period when she could capitalize. When the tourist season finished, everything went dead in the region. Everybody dreaded autumn. It meant no means of survival if you hadn't busted your butt during summer. She was not complaining… she was just exhausted.

By the third day I was dragging my feet to the massage session. It didn't make sense what was happening, but instead of having my days brighten up, they were getting darker and less and less joyful. "Maybe it's the detox," I told myself in a soothing, convincing tone, and "I have to go through it. I paid too much money."

On the fourth day, I was again cooking at high temperature in the oven. I was feeling sick and wanting to die, but I wasn't willing to give up. "What am I aware of?" I asked out loud. My brain was on fire. Nothing reached me. I kept asking, repeating the question to myself over and over. Nothing. I was blank. Strange.

When it was time to lie on the table I noticed a few candles on the opposite wall just above the cosmetics shelf. I made a note to myself that candles always make rooms feel cosier.

My eyes slid to the right where a 2x1 metre roll-up featured the products my masseuse was using on me, along with an image of Anubis, the ancient jackal head god of embalming the dead. I had not seen it before.

In an instant, it all made sense. Like thunder, the information was downloaded into my world. What universe was I tapping into without realizing it? How many entities working for the ancient god were summoned around the massage table every time a body was lying down?

My body sighed with relief. Just like that, the fog around my head dissipated. Once I had acknowledged what I was perceiving, the energy shifted and lightened up.

When I got off the table, I was feeling light and happy, genuinely joyful for living. I completed 14 treatments and celebrated the end of the holidays with a much leaner body and a much lighter mind.

Pearls for Girls

I take a last look in the mirror on the way out. My eyes fall on the pearl necklace resting elegantly around my neck.

"With these pearls, you could be naked and nobody would notice," my husband smiles behind me. "Except for me, of course!"

***

I travelled to Australia a few years ago to attend a class that would certify me as an Access Consciousness® Certified Facilitator. It was my first experience with such a long flight and my husband surprised me with a First Class ticket on Emirates Airlines. In a way, this was a celebration of the choices I had made up to that moment, and all that would come after. There were no words to render my joy, my surprise, and my smallness when all that happened. I had wished for it so much that when my wish was granted, without struggle, and a lot of ease, I didn't think I deserved it.

I remember checking the airline website for the pricing updates. I watched all the presentation videos while I was trying to convince myself that I could not afford this kind of luxury. I was swinging from economy to business class, hardly ever considering First class even though I yearned for that experience. My husband was getting tired of my incessant twisting and turning when I finally asked myself a question: "If money were absolutely no issue, what would I choose?"

"The experience! By far!" That flight is what I call today my biggest leap of faith into receiving in the last 20 years of my life.

When I sat down in the exquisite private cabin on the flight to Dubai, I cried worlds of gratitude expelling the idea that I would not deserve something from my universe. I could have never imagined that "Dom Perignon" would become a girl's best friend on a flight as one of the flight attendants called the fizzy "reserve Champagne".

***

The class had been on for a few days when I asked one of my friends to join me for a walk on the main shopping street in Noosa, Queensland. I wanted to practice with receiving judgments, and ask for what I would really desire. All the shops were looking posh, elegant, and certainly for rich people. It felt as if there was a huge blinking sign above their entrances saying, "Not for you! Keep out." It annoyed me to be licking the windows and not daring to go inside.

There were also a lot of antique shops. They were pulling me in. I could look at the objects in the window and imagine their lives before they landed on display. Strangely, I was particularly attracted by pearls. I had never liked them. I used to think that they were so out of fashion, that only old dried-up spinsters who smell like sweet, heavy powder perfumes would wear them. Yet, there I was, obsessively looking for pearls.

One of the shops had a few stunning strings in a silver and glass cabinet in the window. I braced up and stepped in pretending I was not interested in any of the objects. When I looked around, all I could see were endless strings of pearls - all sizes, types, shapes, and colours. They were hypnotizing. They were all chattering to me at the same time, "Me, me, me!" I hardly knew anything about pearls, their origin, prices, or lustre. Other than the colour or size, I could hardly tell any difference. To me they were all amazingly beautiful and made me want to taste them like tic-tac bonbons.

The lady at the counter was less enthusiastic. She definitely was not in the mood for being bothered by two giggly ladies nosing around in her shop, possibly not closing a deal that day. She showed us a string or two when she decided to ignore us completely.

I, on the other hand, was not done. There was something inside me pulling me to look everywhere for something I didn't know existed.

"Can I see those, please?" I asked when my eyes noticed a beautiful long shiny string of white pearls hanging around the neck of a black velvet doll bust, above the transparent counter on the main wall of the shop. I had been staring at them for a while. The shop manager finally approached me with obvious discontent.

"Oh, those!" She looked up and didn't move one finger. "Yes," I insisted undisturbed. She reluctantly pulled them down. She was holding them in one of the hands, while her other one was checking something on her computer.

"Aren't they beautiful?" she was looking intensely at them, softly playing with the pearls. Her face had changed. Her gaze became distant and absent. She sighed.

"So, can I see them?" I insisted. She pierced me with her eyes, as if her pupils were suddenly flooded by the darkest black I had ever seen in someone's eyes. She composed herself and answered in a professional tone:

"Yes, sure!" and she glided them around her neck two times and continued passing her hand along the string. As if sunk in sadness and nostalgia, she became almost transparent, frail, and helpless in front of my eyes.

The download came unexpectedly: an image of her hung with her pearls. All my hairs stood up on my body. I threw a glance at my friend just to make sure I was not making things up. She was watching the scene in disbelief.

We left the shop silently without uttering a word for a few minutes, trying to make sense of what we had experienced. Of all the strings we wanted to look at and to touch, she put those around her neck. It seemed they were off limits to us.

The download made sense. What if she died in some other lifetime holding on to those pearls? What if they truly belong to her? I had also noticed that our eagerness and insistence to look for pearls dissipated. Until the next day…

***

My group of friends broke for lunch. We were all looking for some time by ourselves. Some took a dive in the ocean, others were having cocktails on a sunny terrace. I went window shopping again. Just around the corner of the venue, a few steps down into a shopping area, in one corner, half hidden by a parasol, there was a jewellery store. It had this delicate, feminine, almost surreal energy to it like you would have to tip-toe inside so not to wake up some magic creature sleeping there. The display was showing a few pearl strings saying simply: Pearls for Girls. I had noticed that the shop had odd hours of operation. I promised myself to check it out the next time I was passing by.

When I stepped over the threshold, a current of air tickled the chimes just above the door announcing my visit. There was no one inside. The air was cool and fresh offering shelter from the heat outside. I found the glass array of jewellery and was fascinated with the candy-like pearls. They all looked like sea fairies resting on coral branches or among shells and rainbow-like seaweed. They invited me to a contemplation moment.

I had been enjoying the view for a while when I perceived another presence in the shop. A man was standing quietly next to me, with his hands behind his back, looking over my shoulder as if he was trying to see what I was perceiving. He smiled at me when I turned myself towards him.

"Welcome," he said in an inviting tone. "Aren't they beautiful? Grains of iridescent shine! It's unbelievable sometimes what beauty Mother Nature is gifting us."

He walks behind the counter and rests his palms on the transparent surface.

"They are absolutely stunning!" I reply. "Thank you for your warm welcome."

"Please take your time. This beauty is not to be rushed. It needs to be cherished. I'll be around. Just let me know if there is anything you would like to ask me about." He vanishes somewhere in the back through an opening.

It seems like time has frozen. I'm sunk in a bubble of ethereal sensations tingling all the cells of my body, awakening it to something… from a different world. My eyes admire each speck of shimmer rolling off the jewellery. I soon discover that I am drawn to the soft hues of golden rosy purple of some of the pearls. A short string of sparkling pearls is blinking at me. Before I could open my mouth, the man is standing in front of me handing me the desired necklace.

"It's a beautiful creation on a gorgeous woman," he said in a soft voice. "You have great taste." He is not just complimenting me. I catch his eyes in the mirror. I see myself in the reflection. My face has changed. It's luminous, relaxed. I could say I have a tan. I take a closer look. They rest perfectly around my neck. I would have never thought that short strings would feel this good.

I hand the string back to him. He sets it aside.

"Maybe you might want to try this one," he offered retrieving a different necklace from the counter. "They are slightly more expensive. The difference is the shape, the size, and the shine they give."

I put them around my neck. My body buzzes and vibrates pleasantly. My head starts spinning.

"It's nice," I said… "but there's something about the other ones, the colours. If I could have a mix of them!"

"Well, I can do that for you. Just tell me which are the pearls that you would like on which necklace."

I am certainly not expecting this. He arranges the strings on a special pallet and awaits my instructions. He removes the clutch of the first one holding a small pair of pliers in his hand.

I point to the pearls I desire and the place in the new string I wish for them to go when I hear myself saying out loud with a sense of emergency and despair:

"Stop! They don't want to be separated! They chose each other for a reason!" A strange relaxation pours in my world. I notice that my shoulders were previously tight and contracted and that my neck had stiffened.

"I know!" the man replied calmly. "I am glad they told it to you too."

"Can I hold them for a moment, please?" I asked hesitantly.

I hold the pearls in my hand. It's a happy, rich feeling. I smile. "So, let's be clear here, if I buy you, will you make me money?"

"Yes!" there were giggles coming from nowhere.

"I'll take them with me, thank you!" I announced the owner of the shop.

"They are in good hands. Thank you for honouring their voice. They will honour you and make you stand out in the crowd. I'll prepare a box for you and the document for the tax deduction. And something else…" He gifts me a pair of gorgeous pearl earrings that match my necklace. "It's a complimentary gift to you. You will love how they match."

***

I remember the man's words. My pearls keep their promise. They do lighten up my world and open energetic doors to receiving I could have never guessed. Pearls are for girls.

India

As the date of departure for my trip to India was drawing closer, I started to observe my moods. I was nervous, then all of sudden happy, then concerned, then worried, then carefree. It was like riding alone on a never-ending rollercoaster.

It would be my second trip to India. I was gifted the first one by the company I used to work for. They had just acquired a European team, and they felt it was important for all divisions to know each other and how they worked, so that they could homogenize general procedures in the long run.

When the plane landed in Bangalore, I stepped onto the bridge connecting the gate to the terminal. A gush of wind reached us through a door. My body reacted instantly: we are home! I felt so elated, so excited, inquiring with curious eyes this experience of a different continent. My feet and legs were vibrating, and I was almost expecting to take off by myself. I was giggling like a child in an amusement park.

Once through the customs check, I connected with my driver. He approached me, asked my name, reached out for my bag, and walked towards the car.

"Hey, wait a minute. What are you doing?" I snatched the bag from his hands.

"I am helping you, ma'am." He answered confused.

"Who are you again?" I asked checking my phone for messages that would confirm his identity.

"I'm Rohnit, ma'am. I'm your driver."

"Why didn't you say so?" I rolled my eyes making a funny face.

"And who is he and why is he following us?" I pointed to the guy following us close.

"That's your security guard ma'am."

"My… what?"

He didn't say anything else. He opened the back door for me to step into the car. The guard was already sitting inside.

"I will sit next to you," I said sliding to the left.

"This is not allowed, ma'am."

"Why not? I want to sit in the front. I want to see everything!" By now the driver was embarrassed. He didn't know what to do. "Sir?" he waited for indications from the guard. He just nodded and made a dismissal sign with his hand indicating I could ride in the front seat of the car.

When I reached the hotel I was advised to take a few hours and allow my body to catch up with the time difference. I tried. There was so much excitement in my world that I could fly. I watched the workers on the site across the street for several minutes when I decided I would take a walk. My business meetings didn't start until the afternoon. I had plenty of time. Time to be home…

***

Now it was time to return to India, not to Bangalore

as before but this time to Mumbai. On my own. There was no ulterior motive involved other than my business with entities. I had chosen, last minute, to take an advanced Talk To The Entities class with Shannon O'Hara. India was calling. After the somewhat idyllic first encounter with the place, its flavours, spices, its colourfully dressed people, unique blue sky, and the upside down moon, I was so eager to revive the experience.

I was carrying with me the scent of the Nilgiri Mountains, the stink of elephants, the flutter of butterflies, the fire flowers, the eyes of a deer that looked me straight in the eyes, and the myriad of birds waking up the wilderness.

That weekend, my work colleague and I took a trip to the Bandipur Tiger Reservation, a paradise on Earth, where elegance and nature walk together. We travelled by car for 7 hours to get there. The driver had received very clear instructions to reach the reservation before 9 pm. If not, we would not get into the camp. Luckily, we made it just in time and when the huge metal gates closed behind us I knew that there must have been a valid reason for the lock down.

I was exhausted. We had travelled like queens, with the greatest comfort possible, but cars are not my favourite means of transport. I stepped out of the car and stretched vigorously. A waiter offered us refreshing towels and fresh grapefruit juice. We were then kindly shown the hut where we were to spend the night.

"Watch your step," said our porter. "Please do not venture off the illuminated path. You never know what is lurking there," he added apologetically.

He opened the door of our bungalow and welcomed us with a bow. I had never seen so much space in a bungalow, nor so much elegance and fancy decoration. It looked like a posh villa with a huge bed in the middle of the room, a bar, a bathroom with an Italian walk-in shower activated by sensors, and a servant's room that was bigger than my own living room. It all was surrounded by glass windows, which seemed quite strange to me until the next morning. I opened my eyes and I fell back on my pillows savouring the surreal scenery.

Our hut was at the far end of the resort. We could see the solid cement fence and the electric wire protecting the people inside. They had told us that the elephants walk past the resort and they wanted to keep them away. Still, nothing had prepared me for the sound of the jungle at night. All the cells of my body were turned on. The air was charged with a strange expectation.

I booked a foot safari by myself the next day. The guide had specifically asked me not to shower, not to put on any perfume, and to wear old clothes. I did, however, brush my teeth. He nodded disappointed. "We'll see what happens," he warned me. We walked to the gates at the far end of the resort. He opened them and made sure they stayed ajar. "Just in case," he added.

The moment he said that my whole body became alert. I was fully and acutely aware of everything. My heart was pounding; my breath was shallow. I turned instantaneously from a civilized person into a hunted animal. My nostrils were wide open ready to catch the faintest movement of air. My ears seemed elongated and tense. My body seemed lighter. My steps were cautious. My eyes were scrutinizing the tall bushes for signs of danger.

"Stop." The guide made a sign for me to not move. A herd of deer ran past us and jumped over the concrete fence, not very tall yet quite wide. Once they were at a fair distance from us, one could have hardly said that there was anything else to be seen.

A small gaggle of blue parrots flew close by. All kinds of information was flooding into my Universe.

"There's an elephant," I said. A few seconds later, we heard the sound reaching us from deep within the bushes.

"He smelled you," said the guide. Anything that is not a natural smell for them is a potential danger.

We walked a bit being on the lookout. A light breeze of air was caressing the bushes making rich sounds. A few steps further, there was an observation post high above a tree. I climbed and melted at the view. My body was heating in the sun, sweat was covering my forehead, and an uncomfortable awareness and expectation of danger was taking hold...

"We have to move, NOW," thundered the guide. He threw me out of the daydreaming of the moment and urged me to walk briskly towards the gate. "He is there… probably 30 metres in the bushes, to your left. He is watching us and is ready to charge." All my sphincters contracted violently. The guide grabbed me by the arm to make sure I was not left behind. I did not dare look behind, yet I surely knew I would not like to be the target of a bull elephant. We made it safely to the gates. The elephant came out of its hiding place right where the guide had predicted it would be. It was close… very close…

I returned to the bungalow and threw myself in

the shower. The intensity of the recent experience overwhelmed me. It was one of the first moments where I acknowledged the degree of awareness one can have in potential dangerous situations and that all those impulses coming from everywhere were what made the Earth. It was all so simple, clear, neat, direct, and expansive.

***

Mumbai strikes me as a very intense and dense city.

When the limo pulled over in front of the hotel I could sense a strange uneasiness creating a weird sensation in my back. It felt like panic, which I tried to mask with a serious expression until I could get my head around it. The porter and the people at the reception were exceptionally polite and helpful, yet my whole body was warning me about… something. I could not grasp it. I realized that what annoyed me the most was the security check at the entrance of the hotel.

It looked like common procedure. I was telling myself that it might be a sign of a well-established brand of hotels offering the guests the highest in terms of safety. I soon forgot about it and my friend and I went up to our room.

The next morning when we came down for breakfast, my eyes were caught by the milky blankness of the air. I was looking outside the huge windows overlooking the bay and I couldn't see a thing. It was as if someone had painted the skies in white. I kept focusing on the vast whiteness until my eyes hurt. In my head, I was still suffering the side effects of my trip – my plane had been delayed, and my friend's flight was as well. I had to wait at the airport for 4 hours until we could both travel to the hotel together.

Indian breakfast is one of my favourite ways to start the day: rich, spicy, and unexpected. My body was giggling with every bite, utterly enjoying the surprises of tastes and flavours. It is not every day that I serve my body a spicy hot variety of masterfully curated vegetables with saffron, cumin, and other delights. It felt like a celebration of the senses.

We were getting ready for a day of adventure in the city. The class wouldn't start until the next day; therefore, we booked an Uber tour of Mumbai. The milky sensation was still there even at lunch. Our driver was skilfully taking us to different sightseeing places in the city. We asked him to take us to a Jain temple and to wait for us.

Stories of the Unseen

The Temple was located on a busy street where it seemed impossible to even stop the car for a moment. We took advantage of a calm instance in the traffic and, together with my friend, we approached the impressively high wooden carved gates. People were quiet. My eyes were itching from the mound of incense burning on the altars. We took off our shoes and were directed to a ragged cupboard where we could find something to cover our heads. No woman was allowed inside if her head was not covered.

Both my friend and I were looking very blonde and European amongst the local population. We were doing our best to become transparent so that no one felt embarrassed around us. We split at the entrance of the Temple, going where the energy was pulling us. It was fascinating to me to watch all these people taking a break to go worship their gods with such devotion, as if their lives depended on it. Some were bowing, some were rocking back and forth, and many of them were reciting mantras with *rudrashka* beads in their hands.

I was so curious as to what and why they were praying. I saw old people and very young ladies absorbed in the praying act. While walking around the temple, I started to think about how ungrateful I was. I looked up. My vision seemed to have recorded the milky white from outside. It was now reconstructing itself inside the temple. I closed my eyes. The next moment my body felt heavy, bulky, and extremely tired. It was as if I didn't have any energy to move. Since there was no place to sit down, I forced myself to walk to an open space.

"How can you just come in and stare at these people? Who do you think you are? You were welcomed here and all you do is criticise? Is this the way to show your gratitude?" My stomach caught fire suddenly. It was burning and cramping and I could hardly stand on my feet. The change was so sudden and violent that I was afraid I might throw up on my way out of the temple. I stormed into the open air, but the thoughts intensified.

"Oh, so this is what you're doing now? Playing the drama queen?" Oh, my tummy, oh... I almost stumbled on one of the monks sweeping the narrow path with a peacock feather fan. I apologized making an awkward face while trying to control my gagging impulses. I grabbed my shoes and ran into the street as fast as I could. My whole body was shaking and my eyes were swollen and red. My throat was hurting from the tension of keeping in my breakfast. My neck felt stiff.

I didn't know what to make of it. I was feeling awful and unworthy to even live on the face of the

Earth. It all seemed so real and righteous, and I was so wrong... I felt almost ashamed to talk about it. Those voices weren't unknown to me, yet it was the first time I heard them so loudly. It was as if the louder they got, the more true they became.

When the drama of the moment settled down, away from the Temple, back in the hotel room, I rewound the whole episode in my head. All of it seemed so real: the panic attack, the guilt, the shame, the blame, the regret, the fear... because all those feelings were so familiar. Then, I got it. Those feelings were being created by demons. And, I was allowing them to make me feel small and unworthy. Not this time!

I was happy because this was the first time I was willing to acknowledge actually being demonized. It couldn't have happened if I had no significance on what I thought demons were. I knew no demon was a match for my bright light. What point of view was I holding onto that allowed demon entities to mess with my life?

There is nothing in this world that can have power over me unless I give away my power, including demons. I found a note pad and wrote down: Do not engage. Clear![7]

The tension faded away. The next morning I was

ready for class.

***

Three days later, the weather had suddenly changed in Delhi. The taxi driver who took us from the airport to the hotel was friendly and chatting with us. In 40 minutes we learned everything about his family, extended family, wedding plans, hard work, and his living on little money. In between, we had the chance to tell him our plans and that we would like to see the Taj Mahal.

"Not a good time, madam. Not good. It's misty. These days you go all the way over there and you might not see it. Too much mist, madam, too much mist."

Later that day we booked our trip to the Agra Fort and Taj Mahal, regardless of the opinions of the people we met. We kind of felt empowered to receive the contribution from the entities for which we had travelled all the way to India to receive.

We started off early in the morning with our train ride to Agra. It was a fun experience to be the only blondes on the train and perceive peoples' curiosity. As our guide explained later, for many of them, we were a bad omen, and for others, we were a divine sign. Things began to take a very strange twist the moment when people asked us to take pictures with them. We suddenly became curious tourist attractions.

I remember being very close to Agra when the train stopped abruptly without warning. Nobody else seemed to panic except for us. The conductor passed by and announced: "There's mist in Agra. We don't know how long it will take to clear up. Yesterday we were stopped for 4 hours."

I threw a glance to my friend and agreed silently that we were not having that. We lowered our barriers and we asked all conscious entities to assist us and the train to reach the destination in time for us to continue our visit. We also acknowledged that they have already been a huge contribution, and that it was time to speed up the things a bit. We both laughed. If anyone had any idea what we were doing, they would have called us insane.

It took 5 minutes to produce a bit of magic and divine intervention. Soon, the train started off. Actually, its early arrival startled our driver who was supposed to take us to The Taj Mahal. When the authorities announced that we were delayed, he had snuck into a coffee shop to chat with his friends. He could hardly believe that we made it on time.

The Taj Mahal is nothing like I expected it to be. It went beyond my imagination and way deeper into what I knew about its history. Majestic, elegant, and sad, its white marble shines from hundreds of meters in the distance. It is not only the architectural refined audacity and the breath-taking scenery that mesmerizes everybody, but also the revitalizing energies gravitating around the mausoleum of Mumtaz.

When we approached the main Eastern gate my heart sank. There was an emptiness and sadness, as if I could not fully enjoy the beauty of the view without being reminded of the sacrifices of the families and labourers who had been working there for generations. The legend says that it was Mumtaz Mahal who asked her husband, Shah Jahal, to build her the monument at her death as a symbol of his love. She had given him 14 children and died during the last birth.

"Are you sisters?" This was probably the 4th time someone asked us this. In some strange way we might have been sharing a sisterhood in some other lifetime, but this life we could not be more different. The guide looked at us with inquiring eyes. "You certainly resemble each other!" We smiled at the funny idea and continued to queue in front of the entrance of the imperial tomb.

Inside, it was as if I had entered an empty blackness. My eyes were basking in the beauty and craftsmanship of all the delicate carvings and intricate inlays of precious stones while the rest of my body was carried by the masses towards the exit. We only had 10 minutes to admire the tombs when we were rushed outside. There was a continuous flood of tourists compelling the guards to brutally ask us to get out. I actually appreciated being allowed to leave the place.

Once outside, I was almost blinded by the sun reflecting off of the white marble walls and off of the ground. I sat down for a minute trying to figure out that empty darkness. Where was it coming from?

My friend finally appeared in the arch of the exit door. She looked radiant, happy, and ecstatic.

"This is gorgeous! Amazing! You can feel her presence! Wow!"

I looked at her puzzled.

"Well, there was nothing for me in there, just… empty darkness…"

"Oh, my god, I felt the connection with her! So

strong, so powerful, what a potent lady she was!"

I kept silent, annoyed that I was possibly not good enough, not aware enough, not worthy enough to have experienced this kind of connection. I knew that I was being pulled in by the monument, and that there was way more for me to discover. I felt frustrated that all I could report was: nothing.

We continued our journey to Agra. We hopped on a *tuc-tuc* and enjoyed the sheer craziness of the busy village. Everybody was honking. We were almost touching people on their bicycles with our knees. It was insane to trust our driver, but he surely knew what he was doing and we were laughing loudly. The farther from the monument we got, the happier I felt.

Agra Fort… there was a warmth engulfing my body ever since we crossed the bridge to the main entrance. I don't recall the stories or the legend of this place, but the atmosphere marked a vivid impression in my awareness. It was as if I knew where the rooms of the fort were and where Mumtaz had lived with her husband. I could perceive the lust, the kindness, the caring, the nurturance, and the sexualness imprinted in the thick walls of the fort. The guide kept talking. I kept ignoring him.

All of a sudden, tears were gushing from my eyes. A deep sorrow, a lifetime of suffering and despair, all poured out of my eyes. I was sobbing and gasping for air while looking through a carved marble fence. I could see the Taj Mahal in the distance. The sight sent needles up my spine.

To my left, far from my peripheral vision, a man was sitting facing the monument. He had no details to him, just this defeated posture and engrained sadness. I felt helpless. There was a part of me who was desperately trying to soothe that presence, to hug it, and to let it cry on my shoulders. I couldn't… It felt as if I had been doing this for a long time, and every time I would look to my left I had this insistent hope that everything would be all right… although I knew it wouldn't be.

"And," the guide is pointing a finger towards a kind of balcony coming out of the main building – "this is the place where Shah Jahal was forced in house arrest by his son. He was locked up shortly after the monument was finished. He was forbidden to leave his room. He didn't want to anyway. The only thing that he had left was to look at his wife's tomb every day," continued the guide in a monotonous tone, walking past me.

My sadness dissipated. My body relaxed. My breath

calmed down, and my mind was at peace. What was I aware of? What gift had been this trip to Agra? Awareness flooded in my world, like a storm of liquid knowing. I was no longer resisting it.

"Are you sisters?" a boy was looking at us amused, and making signs to his mom to come closer. She approached shyly.

"No, we are not. Not in this lifetime…"

I couldn't help but wondering if this trip had reconnected us with our family… The legend says that one of the daughters of the couple was dedicated to her mother while the other one had sworn to serve her father…

Was it time to release all my commitments from any other lifetime and bring more choice in what seemed a worldwide, cherished, sad, love story?

***

India has surpassed itself. It is always intense and intriguing. I am now killing some time before my flight takes off from Delhi, flipping through my phone. An article title catches my attention: "Hotel Mumbai, former Taj Mahal Palace". I click on it. As I do, all becomes clear: the security checks, the uneasiness, the paranoid feeling inside the hotel. My body finally relaxes and releases the edginess I previously experienced. I become weightless for a second. What gift have I been to this place that I hadn't been aware of?

Mexico

I am watching the Uber drive up the alley close to the apartment building I had stayed at in Puerto Vallarta. My bags are ready for the return flight to Belgium. I am not. There is this unnerving feeling of things left unspoken, unfinished. I keep rolling my tongue in my mouth as if I was looking for something forgotten between my teeth. I wish I could stay a little longer.

"Laptop, check. Passport, check. Headphones, check. Wallet, check. Big luggage, small luggage, shoulder bag, check." Everything seems to be fine.

I jump inside the car and as soon as I close the door, the driver starts on the way to the airport. There's a 23 hour flight journey in front of me. I am a bit apprehensive. "What have I forgotten?" My mind cannot settle. My body feels anxious and impatient.

After the security check I make my way to the gate. I still have 2 hours to spend doing nothing. I linger a while in the souvenir shops. There is not much I could buy. I am already overloaded. I end up in an Urban Caffé just across from the boarding gate.

Time seems to have dissolved in Puerto Vallarta. People take their time. They have fun, laugh, and add 'gimme one second' which in everyone's understanding reads 'I'll be back when I'll be back!' I wait by the entrance sign until it is my turn to be seated. A quick glance on the menu makes my stomach contract. I do the math: 1h30 until departure, 1h30 connecting time in Mexico City, an 11 hour flight to Amsterdam, a 6 hour lay over, and another 40 minute flight to Brussels. It's a long way to skip eating at this point.

There's a short and lean smiling guy standing next to me ready to take my order. I choose the less 'harmful' option from what I could find on the menu. My body is not happy. I know it from the cringe in the stomach.

"Just gimme a second, lady!" and he disappears.

Selena Ardelean

***

I take my phone out and flip through the pictures of my stay in Puerto Vallarta.

I stop breathing for a moment. There is this nude of me taken during a photoshoot. It's me, mesmerizing me. I scrutinize the picture. I realize I cannot judge it. I am grateful for it. It's a new and surprising way of being to me.

That, however, was one of those instances in time where there was no judgment in my world. I was lying naked on a floor of an ordinary apartment, with several pairs of eyes riveted over me and a camera. I was beautifully vulnerable, gorgeously embarrassed by my own magic.

A few moments earlier, during that photo shoot, I had caught a glimpse of a different frame. It had made me viscerally sick. Demons from a long forgotten past resurged out of nowhere.

"I hate that picture!" I said out loud, throwing my head back as if mortified by the view.

"Do you?" The photographer paused for a moment.

"Do I?...Well, I don't, but this is the 'face' that people

tend to judge the most when they see it. I look horrible there."

"Do you? What if instead of judging this picture you would be willing to be grateful for the gift it is? Without this shot, none of the following ones could have existed. What if every picture is an entity willing to gift to you and to contribute to your life with every molecule they touch, change, and shift for more consciousness? Would you be willing to receive their gift?"

"I would have to acknowledge me as being a gift before I can receive anything at all…" My eyes welled up with a storm of emotions. All those places where I had learned to judge myself, to push through walls and barriers, to force, to control, to think… were melting.

The eye of the camera opened wide and barely perceptible energies began to dance behind the glass. With every flash, flickers of possibilities and universes of play and curiosity were pouring out, enveloping my body and exploding like ticklish fireworks inside me. Alive, turned on, and utterly vulnerable…I opened to a new space of receiving from entities.

***

My food arrived 35 minutes later. My tummy is not happy with the sight of the dish. I take a bite and I can hardly swallow it. I try another one in an effort to convince myself that I am wise about eating now and to not wait until the connecting flight. There's no way I can wash the terrible food down my throat. There's nothing wrong with it. It's just not for me today. Within 10 minutes I am paying for my order and holding tight to my bottle of mineral water.

***

The skull tattoo on the waiter's arm takes me back to the rooftop pool of the apartment building I have been staying at for the past two weeks. I smile. The waiter's name is Rodrigo.

I had just returned from one of the classes, exhausted and happy. My body was longing for water. I ditched the sweaty clothes and slipped into my bathing suit.

"I could use a glass of wine," I mumble.

From high up, the marina was sunk in darkness, but Puerto Vallarta was inflamed by twinkling lights. Music reached my ears from the cafés open until late at night. Bodies are alive!

The giggles in the pool catch my attention: 5 ladies

are enjoying the cool breeze of the early night. They splash and tease each other speaking fast and dirty, judging by their laughs. I don't speak Spanish, yet I get the gist of their conversation. When they see me they take distance from one another. Suspicion invades the waters.

"Hi, I'm Selena. Don't mind me. I don't speak Spanish, so you're safe with me. I won't tell what I see!" I wink and swim to the other side of the pool. We all laugh.

"No, no, no… not Selena Gomez and not the dead one," I added, reading their minds.

"You're psychic!" one of them exclaims.

"Sometimes, but in this case it's more of a habit! Mexicans love Selena's," I add emphatically. "No, I don't sing either!" The evening air resonates with our laughter.

They have been friends for years and are having a weekend away from their families. Their children are grown-ups and call them all aunties. I am fascinated with their thirst for life.

"What is your secret to look so good?" I ask.

"Tequila and hot men," answers the oldest one. "You should try," she continues. "Maybe we can teach you how to drink properly." We all burst out laughing.

"What do you do in life?" The question floats above the water.

"I talk to entities," the words flow out of my mouth.

"Oh, you too?" the laughter is unbearable.

We talk about 'calaveras', the sugary skulls Mexicans offer to the families on Dia de Los Muertos (the Day of The Dead) to celebrate life and to remember the dead ones in a sweet way. We talk about Frida Kahlo and José Guadalupe Posada's La Catrina - the dandy woman skeleton made of clay or wood or papier-mâché dressed up elegantly and wearing hats and feathers, the fashion of skull tattoos, and about the movie Coco. And yes, they do believe that when there is no one else left on Earth to celebrate and remember them, their soul will disappear, just like in the movie. But until then, life is a celebration, so live it!

***

"Hola, chica!"

I turn my head all of a sudden in an attempt to identify whether I am 'the chica' and where the sound is coming from. My friends are walking in front of me through the galleria caught up in a discussion about lunch preference. I am searching inside my bag for my phone, distracted by the call. The voice was deep, manly, and seductive.

There is no one around me. There are only a few tables filled with craft works which are left unattended. "I must have been imagined it!"

"Here!"

I look down from where the sound appears to come.

"Hi!" I reach to the small calavera (skull) on the edge of the table, finely decorated with silver, black, and gold beads, and with intricate patterns on it.

I grab the skull from the top and I jolt with surprise when its jaw drops. My friends approach. A deep playful and macho voice resonates in my ears. It moans mostly. I giggle and I feel like a cheeky teenager. The skull's white and grey pattern on the teeth invite me to play. And we do! There's a conversation pouring out with me changing voices and having fun with these new discovered energies.

"Who's that?" asks one of my friends.

"Rodrigo!" I answered immediately.

"How do you know?" they burst into laughter.

"He told me!" my voice changes and Rodrigo comes to play. He's a hunk, a charmer, a player.

"How much for the skull?" I finally ask the owner of the table.

"*$35*"

"Too much" I replied setting the skull on the table and we went for lunch.

On the way back to the apartment, Rodrigo is winking at me from the table.

"Listen, handsome, what's your price?" I asked the skull.

"$20," it replied instantly.

"Will you make me money if I buy you?" I continued, making sure I'm in for a good deal.

"You pay $20, I'll bring 100 times more".

"Fair enough!"

I carry Rodrigo in my hand up to the apartment laughing and talking to it. There's an energy I recognize from when I was a child and I learned how to play with puppets. It was a good cover up for the voices I was hearing in my head. Today, however, I know I am not inventing the voices. Sometimes they are loud, and sometimes they buzz my ears with their silence.

PS. Rodrigo is a neat guy. He always keeps his end of the deal. He brought me 200 times more money in the next days and was very stoked to contribute to all of my classes.

***

"Body, are we getting sick? Is this what this is all about?" I know we're not, I just need to make sure I am prepared in case of an emergency. With the corner of the eye I catch the message next to the information concerning the departures. My flight to Mexico City is delayed by 30 minutes. "We're all good." Time flies and I don't mind the extra time for using the Wi-Fi connection of the airport.

I fall asleep soon after take-off. The flight attendant's voice announcing our arrival plunges me back to reality: "It's 7:58pm local time." My body shivers. I take a look at the boarding card for the connection: gate closes at 8:50pm. I know I will not make it in time. Still, I am compelled to rush.

It feels like the world is in slow motion. My feet could catch up, but the people around me are not. I finally reach the gate at 9:05 pm. Gate closed, flight gone. I'm angry, not with missing the flight but with the slow pace this world is revolving at. The last gate agent sends me back to the terminal I had just been rushing from to rebook my flight and arrange accommodation for the night. I'm steaming with frustration. No one has been capable of giving me reliable information when it came to instructions on how to navigate the way to the terminal, and it's humongous!

Three hours later after landing and after an extra covid test, I am resting on a queen size bed in the hotel just across the terminal. It smells like humidity and old dirt. I smile, "Hello, my friends, anyone care to talk to me?" I giggle and I fall asleep dressed from the road.

It's 7:00am. I jump out of my bed and grab my phone. I google "Téotihuacan Pyramids", and a rush of energy pours through every cell of my body! I am excited and restless… and I know. Ever since I planned my trip to Mexico, I had wanted to visit the pyramids but somehow the travel arrangements didn't fall into place… or so I thought. It's a 45 minute drive to the site. My flight leaves late in the evening. Yes, I can make it back and forth. Yes, with ease, please.

I draw the heavy occulting curtains and let the sun burn my retinas. I recall my agitated sleep, being constantly cold and trembling under the covers. I take a shower and rush down to the reception desk. A taxi can take me to the pyramids and the driver will wait for me to do the tour. How did I get so lucky? I can perceive a whole bunch of excited entities behind me. "Just make sure we make it there with ease and back on time, please!" I say it out loud. The receptionist raises an eyebrow. "Oh, sorry, I was just talking to myself!"

I've been sitting quietly in the car for a few long moments. My neck is hurting, my head looks for a relief position and it's thrown far back, hanging low on my back. I might look quite strange through the rearview mirror. The tension descends down my spine burning my shoulder blades and accumulating in my lower back. My tailbone is vibrating painfully. I readjust my body to soothe the tension. It feels familiar and uncomfortable.

"Here it is, the Sun Pyramid of Teotihuacán, where the gods made man." The driver points to his right. It takes me a few seconds to adjust my vision. It's blurry. My eyes are hurting. "And that's the Pyramid of the Moon," he adds. I see it immediately. My heart is pumping; my breath accelerates.

Farther down the road, he takes the car close to the entrance of the archaeological site. He will wait for me and my friend to complete our tour. We step out of the vehicle. The heat is debilitating. Right in front of us, the Pyramid of the Sun is dominating earth and sky at the same time. We approach quietly. Street vendors invite us to souvenirs. They are everywhere on each side of the "Avenue of the Dead."

My eyes are stuck to the Pyramid of the Sun. My mind melts. I sit down on the stairs facing the pyramid in the distance. No one is allowed to step on top of them. I'm relieved. I can have it all for myself while not having to possess it.

The intensity in my back turns into a heat wave, rising from my feet up to the crown. It's like liquid fire is flowing through my spine. My butt is burning on the stones; my face is devoured by the sun of the day; my being is purged in the intensity of it all. I surrender. There's something I came here to receive: a blessing, a question, and a knowing. I feel like my feet are part of the stone, melting and flowing down the joints of the square bricks. I am one with the volcanic rocks building the pyramid, with the volcano behind, and with the river underneath. I am forged again in the fire of creation with the earth.

When the temperature becomes unbearable for my butt I stand up and face the Pyramid of the Moon. The avenue seems huge. I walk right in the middle of it. Every step I take makes the Pyramid of the Moon grow larger. There's a cold breeze cooling down my body. I take out my shoes and walk on the volcano pebbles. Threads of grass, pointy grains of stone, the sound the vendors make with their gadgets, obsidian objects glowing mysteriously in the blinding sun... I walk thoughtless as if hypnotized by the edifice in front of me. I wonder... how many lifetimes have I been sacrificed on those steps? Many. I'm grateful. Strangely I acknowledge that it was a choice I made back then and that today I am honouring those past choices by receiving them and the futures I have been creating. They all allowed me to be here today.

There's a totally different energy to the Pyramid of the Moon. It's smoother, somehow refreshing, sheltering. I know now why I had missed my flight.

It's time to leave. There are clouds rushing in from

all sides. I smile. I've been in Mexico for 2 weeks and I hadn't seen a drop of rain, until I reached Mexico City. We get into the car just in time to not get wet. I remember the shaman in Machu Picchu telling me that all big changes and transformations are blessed by the gods with rain. What a gift!

On the way back I listen to the driver's voice and I drift away. The very first thought that came to my mind when I started planning this trip was to visit the pyramids. But plans don't work, we do! I asked the Universe, and it delivered in a totally unexpected way. And, on my mom's birthday… speaking of receiving from entities… What if what I had forgotten was to acknowledge what a gift my entity awareness is? Thank you! I would like more of this please!

Afterword

Infinitely grateful...

I poured myself a cup of coffee. The sun tickles my nose. I've been on an awareness journey ever since the entities nudged me to put these lines on paper. It has been an intensive exercise in acknowledging the weirdness unique to me and receiving it.

Writing a book is a cooperation process with the energy about to be birthed and its entity. I laughed; I cried; I missed places, people, and creatures; I recalled pains and moments of awe, and most of all, I opened the door to more of me. It didn't show up the way I thought it would. The stories asked to be written by themselves.

For a long time, I thought that I had to write a Romanian story as well. My ancestors are, after all, buried in Romanian ground. "That country has been my home for more than half of my life," my logic said. That story never presented itself to me. I couldn't find the words. They kept sliding, slipping, and dissolving from my world. I am that story, undefined, sliding, slipping, and continuously unfolding, tracing the whispers of awareness I've heard and didn't trust as a child.

I only have this image that wants to be revealed on these pages: the oak tree from my parents' cemetery. Old, strong, and protective, the one I always found shelter under when I went to visit my parents' grave. I've known it since I was a little girl and my family was celebrating the 1st of November at the cemetery, honouring their dead.

Playful and naughty, the entities would blow away all the candles people were struggling to light in memory of the beloved ones. I remember walking through the graves and hopping over some where I knew 'nobody was home'. Some others I would avoid as the 'inhabitants' would not have me come close. Some were creepy. Some were welcoming. On some I would sit listening to the voices of the oak tree.

"You cannot do this! Stop it!" my mom would scold me. To me it was as if people were forcing the dead to stay in this world, all the while pretending that they were at peace with their dying. They were not. The oak tree was somehow my ally and my friend through all of that.

They cut that tree down a few years ago. And I haven't visited Baia Mare since. But it is here, with me, every day, painted in childlike colours, vivid and sprinkled with glitters, as the magical tree it truly is.

What if honouring your dead is not only about bringing flowers to their graves, being desperate with their leaving, lighting up a candle, mourning, and killing ourselves with grief, but also acknowledging that some of them are still around us, some seek to communicate with us, and some others rely on us to ask a question that would open different paths for them?

What if we honoured their choice of leaving instead of holding onto them? What if their choice to stay around us and contribute to us was no longer a wrongness? What if being aware of them is the biggest gift you can offer yourself and to them? What if we could invite them to choose further? They are around every moment of the day, whether we would like to know it or not. Will you invite more ease in your life by acknowledging you are aware of their presence?

What kindness are you to the unseen world that you have not yet acknowledged? And what kindness of entities are you now willing to receive that will heal, shift, and transform all energies with ease?

***

Thank you, mom! I wanted you to go away so badly. I was so furious with you. I was hurt and full of sorrow… yet, you are the one entity that invited me to acknowledge that which you were not allowed to: awareness. The tears I am crying right now are not mine, but an acknowledgment of you. I'll see you under the cherry tree, and when you're not going to be there, I'll know you made a different choice. So be it.

Thank you, my friend! Yes, YOU, the one reading these lines, for you give a sense to my words. I know that you glide over these pages thanks to someone from the unseen world who would have liked you to know that you are beautiful, gorgeous, and awesomely aware. Yet, this is but one of your invaluable gifts, one of the shiniest sparkles, one flash of intense light in this world, and one invitation to consciousness and an inclusive world.

Thank you, Shannon O'Hara and Talk To The Entities® for all the amazing tools that make life much more ease and less significant.

Thank you Gary Douglas and Dr. Dain Heer for the tools of Access Consciousness® that permeate my life and allow me to be more of who I am with every choice I am making.

Thank you, Kalpana, for having poured your kindness into my world and opening the door to more of what I knew was possible.

Thank you, Fay and Sandra, for magically giving form and flow to the unseen world and for honouring it with your gifts.

Thank you, Silvian, Bruno, Sacha and Jeremy for co-creating our life together, from acknowledgment, question, and ask.

Thank you, curious eyes and wandering hearts, so brave to venture on the first draft of this book: Yvonne, Freeke, Oana, Aysegul.

Thank you, disembodied entities, all of you contributing every day to a larger more conscious life and living. Receiving is not logical, neither is it linear. You keep reminding me of this!

Infinitely grateful…

End Notes

[1] To learn more about Talk to the Entities classes, visit www.talktotheentities.com

[2] To learn more about Access Consciousness visit www.accessconsciousness.com

[3] To learn more about the Beings of Light, you can read *Beings of Light*, a book by Shannon O'Hara.

[4] To learn more about the Antique Guild visit www.antiqueguild.com.au

[5] You can purchase the demon clearing audio at http://bit.ly/2kG3L2a

[6] To learn more about Access Bars visit www.accessconsciousness.com/bars

[7] To learn more about clearing demons, visit www.talktotheentities.com

About the Author

Selena Ardelean was born in Romania and immigrated to Belgium in 2004 to be with her husband. She always had big dreams and worked hard to achieve them. In fact, she viewed life as something you had to work for, struggle with, and persevere.

Selena's life reached a turning point after she received a session of Access Bars. From that moment on, she recognized and acknowledged the joy of life, laughter, and ease. She set out to share this with as many people on the planet that would have it.

She began taking classes with Access Consciousness® which led her becoming a facilitator of Talk to the

Entities®. This opened her up to the unseen world of spirit that she always knew was there.

She founded Shine Bright, a company dedicated to making people SHINE in every aspect of their lives. She also loves to facilitate others in acknowledging their awareness of entities and releasing the significance that we attach to them.

Selena lives in Brussels, Belgium with her husband and three children and enjoys life to the fullest whether it be from world travel or a simple cup of coffee.

For more information about Selena and her work, visit:

Website: www.shinebright.be
Facebook: facebook.com/selenardelean
Instagram: @selena_ardelean

For all listings of Selena's Access Consciousness and Talk to the Entities classes visit:

www.accessconsciousness.com/ar/public-profiles/selena-ardelean/

www.ingramcontent.com/pod-product-compliance
Lightning Source LLC
Chambersburg PA
CBHW021424070526
44577CB00001B/43